WOMEN OF POLYNESIA

50 YEARS OF POSTCARD VIEWS
1898 - 1948

MARK BLACKBURN

4880 Lower Valley Road, Atglen, PA 19310 USA

D0814186

DEDICATION
To Sophlonie Williams, a woman of Polynesia,
who gave us the greatest gift of all, our son,
Kuhane Pahanui Blackburn

All images and text in this book are the expressed personal property of Mark and Carolyn Blackburn of Kamuela, Hawaii. They are not to be reproduced in any manner without the full written permission of the author.

All postcards and other images used to illustrate this book are from the personal collection of Mark and Carolyn Blackburn, Kamuela, Hawaii.

Published by Schiffer Publishing Ltd.
4880 Lower Valley Road
Atglen, PA 19310
Phone: (610) 593-1777; Fax: (610) 593-2002
E-mail: Info@schifferbooks.com
For the largest selection of fine reference books on this and related subjects, please visit our web site catalog at www.schifferbooks.com
We are always looking for people to write books on new and related subjects. If you have an idea for a book, please contact us at the above address.

Designed by "Sue"
Type set in Humanist521 BT

ISBN: 0-7643-2174-9
Printed in China

This book may be purchased from the publisher.
Include $3.95 for shipping. Please try your bookstore first.
You may write for a free catalog.

In Europe, Schiffer books are distributed by
Bushwood Books
6 Marksbury Ave. Kew Gardens
Surrey TW9 4JF England
Phone: 44 (0)20 8392-8585; Fax: 44 (0)20 8392-9876
E-mail: info@Bushwoodbooks.co.uk
Free postage in the UK. Europe: air mail at cost.
Please try your bookstore first.

Contents

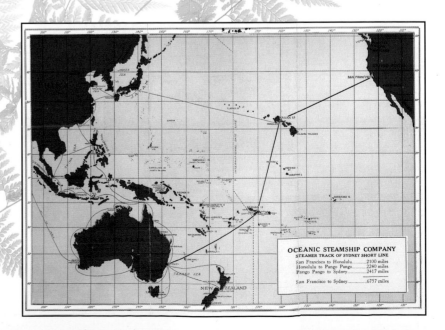

OCEANIC STEAMSHIP COMPANY
STEAMER TRACK OF SYDNEY SHORT LINE
San Francisco to Honolulu..........2100 miles
Honolulu to Pango Pango..........2240 miles
Pango Pango to Sydney..........2417 miles

San Francisco to Sydney..........6757 miles

4

Introduction

The images in the following pages represent a long passion with all things **Polynesian**. In over 25 years of collecting I have gathered over 15,000 postcards from Polynesia with the following representing just a very small portion of our collection. Postcards have always fascinated me because of the way the images have been contextually presented. Like photographs, postcards allow the present day viewer to look not only into the past but also into the social mores and prevailing attitudes of the time period. Not only do these "time capsules" allow the viewer this opportunity but they also allow a small glimpse into the mind of the person or persons in the image.

For the commercial photographer and postcard publisher, portraits illustrating the exotic and picturesque customs and costumes of little known people found a ready market. The increase in the strategic importance of many of these Pacific Islands along with the rapid increase in tourism also added to the desire for these exotic views.

Although in many cases the subjects were placed into a supposedly "natural setting", there were many instances, such as Tahiti, that photographers endeavored to shoot their subjects in a lush and verdant tropical paradise. Correct attention to detail did not concern either the general public or commercial interests involved, often resulting in the inter-mixing of cultures through studio props etc.

Thus the majority of the cards illustrated in this book were inspired by "the noble savage" concept that so fascinated armchair travelers since the time of contact in the 18th century. This concept advanced by the Swiss French philosopher Jean-Jacques Rosseau (1712-1778) helped to create the perception of a heavenly paradise where prevailing social mores and values of modern civilization did not exist. In some areas though such as Hawaii and New Zealand - cards of island women were simply a very early attempt at a type of tourist advertising using exotic views of women to entice travelers to the islands. Whatever the concept that led to the production of these cards. I think you will agree, as did the famed artist Paul Gauguin, *"The Maoris are a noble race..."*

Kamuela, Hawaii
October, 2004

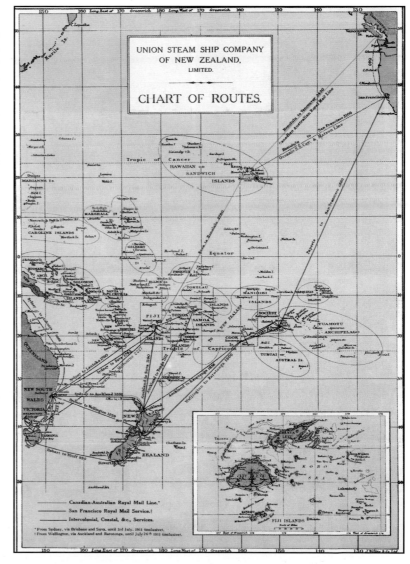

The Cook Islands

Real photo postcard entitled "A Dusky Maid," circa 1920. Photographer unknown.

Real photo postcard by Sydney Hopkins, Rarotonga, circa 1925.

Real photo postcard by Sydney Hopkins, Rarotonga, circa 1925. A rather provocative card for this time period.

The population of the Cook Islands is a little under 20,000 inhabitants.

Chapter 1

The Cook Islands

The Cook Islands consist of fifteen islands scattered over one million square miles of the Pacific. Located at the center of the Polynesian triangle, they are flanked by Tonga and Samoa and to the east by French Polynesia. Falling into two main areas, the northern group consists of low lying coralline atolls with crystal clear lagoons and fringing reefs. The Southern group with the capital and main island of Rarotonga at the center consist of "high" volcanic islands.

Settled in a wave of Polynesian migration around 800 A.D. from Raiatea, the islands were first sighted by Spanish Captain Alvaro de Mendana, in 1595. There was no further contact for over 150 years until the voyages of Captain James Cook, for whom the island group was eventually named. But despite being the namesake of the group, Captain Cook noted in his journals that he personally only went ashore on the small, un-inhabited atoll of Palmerston. The islands were named the Hervey Islands after the Lord of the Admiralty until 1824 when the Russian cartographer Von Krusentstern changed the name in honor of Captain Cook. The famed Reverend John Williams of the London Missionary Society landed in Aitutaki in 1821 and Rarotonga in 1823, and succeeded within a very short time of converting the natives to Christianity.

In 1888 Rarotonga and the islands of Southern group became part of the British Dominion when Captain Edmund Bourke hoisted the British flag. Later, in the year 1901, an Imperial Order of the New Zealand Parliament allowed the annexation of the entire Cook Islands to New Zealand. In 1965 New Zealand signed an order declaring the islands a self-governing state. Today they look to New Zealand for continuing aid since tourism, being their only source of income, is relatively small and only partially developed.

Because of their relatively small size and isolation off the main shipping lanes there was not a huge demand for postcards and photographs in the Cook Islands. The picture postcards were published by firms located in nearby Tahiti and New Zealand, thus making cards from the islands relatively scarce.

Real photo postcard by Sydney Hopkins, Rarotonga, circa 1925. Here a dancer is shown with her costume inspired by the Maori people of New Zealand.

A card depicting women in missionary inspired dress at Avarua Rarotonga. Publisher unknown, circa 1910.

Former iron monger and London missionary, Reverend John Williams, came up with the idea of using converted Polynesians to spread the Gospel to the islands in the west. He sent two natives from Raiatea to Aitutaki, in 1821, and others followed shortly after to Mitiaro, Mangaia, Mauke, and Atiu. Shortly after, Rarotonga fell to these new beliefs with the final burning of the "idols" in 1823. Today, religion remains an integral part of Cook Island culture, with Presbyterian being the main denomination.

Black pearl farming has become a major export within the last few years and is competing with nearby French Polynesia.

Real photo postcard by Sydney Hopkins, Rarotonga, circa 1925.

Real photo postcard by Sydney Hopkins, Rarotonga,, circa 1925.

9

Real photo postcard entitled " Three Native Women of Rarotonga in Holiday Attire," circa 1920. Photographer unknown.

In the Cook Islands' Maori language, there are 14 letters including the glottal stop, which is written as an inverted apostrophe.

Real photo postcard by Sydney Hopkins, Rartonga, circa 1925.

Real photo postcard entitled "Group of Rarotonga Natives out for a Holiday," circa 1920. Photographer unknown. You can see clearly in photos such as this the strict dress codes that were put in place by the missionaries. Here all the women are dressed in the long dresses known throughout Polynesia as "Mother Hubbards."

Bathing Pool, Rarotonga.

A card depicting native beauties in a bathing pool. Publisher unknown, printed in Saxony, circa 1910.

The entire land area of the Cook Islands is approximately 1.3 times the size of Washington D.C.

GROUP OF NATIVE WOMEN OF RAROTONGA RETURNING FROM A HOLIDAY No. 3236.

Real photo postcard, circa 1920. Publisher unknown.

Real photo postcard entitled "Group of Native Women of Rarotonga returning from a Holiday," circa 1920. Photographer unknown.

Published in Milan Italy for the firm of Arthur Mills, circa 1907. There is no evidence that Arthur Mills was a photographer himself. Having arrived from Sydney in 1904 he soon had a thriving business selling a variety of general goods and merchandise. Recorded as suffering from acute anxiety, he committed suicide in 1910.

Typical Fijian Girl.

Very early card of "Adi Cakobau," publisher unknown, circa 1900, with inscription on reverse, "A descendant of the late King Cakobau." Non-divided back.

Fijian Iles

The Fiji Islands

Published by Henry Marks and Co. Ltd, Suva, circa 1907. The Marks firm was considered one of the largest wholesale and retail merchants in the Western Pacific with numerous branches located throughout the Fijian Islands. The firm operated its own fleet of steamers and launches and controlled the lucrative copra trade in Fiji. It also served as agents for many overseas firms. Many of their branches operated as Government post offices adding to the firms ever increasing postcard trade.

Fiji has a population of approximately 870,000. 51 percent of them are indigenous Fijian, 44 percent are of Indian origin.

Chapter 2

The Fiji Islands

Originally called "The Cannibal Islands" by early visitors, due to the inhabitants' lust for human flesh, the country consists of nearly 300 islands, of which less than 100 are populated today. The islands range from high sub-continental landmasses to bright blue lagoon coral atolls and were settled approximately 3,000 years ago from neighboring Samoa and Tonga. Termed "Lapita people," these early settlers' language was of Austronesian origin.

The islands were first sighted in 1643 by the Dutch explorer Abel Tasman, but were left unexplored until the arrival of Captain James Cook who passed thru in 1784. It was Captain William Bligh while searching for the original mutineers in 1789 who is credited with opening the islands to the west. During the latter part of the 18th and early 19th centuries many sandalwood and *beche de mer* traders met their death at the hands of the ferocious inhabitants. Christian missionaries soon followed with their greatest accomplishment the conversion of the paramount chief Ratu Senu Cakobau in 1854, eliminating most intertribal warfare and cannibalism.

Hereditary tribal chiefs watching this approaching colonialism, decided in 1874 to collectively associate with Great Britian – becoming a crown colony. In 1879 the British government along with local planters decided to import indentured laborers from India to work the vast sugar plantations, which continued until 1916 when the system was abolished. Many of these people of Indian descent still remain in the islands today, which has led to a clash of cultures between these two groups. In 1970 the islanders elected to become an independent nation, but remain closely linked to the Commonwealth.

As with other areas of the Pacific, colonial interests soon led to a vast array of picture postcards being produced. The first recorded postcards of Fijian subject matter appeared on the market in 1899 with the firm of Raphael Tuck and Sons Ltd. of London publishing a small series, which was very well received. Soon photographers and publishers in Fiji, Samoa, New Zealand, Australia, Italy, France, United States, and Germany started production. Like Samoa and Tonga the subject matter consisted of *kava* drinking, bark cloth manufacturing, and "savage" sights with cannibalism and inter tribal warfare a popular and unique subject of Fijian origin. Like other areas in the Pacific, very few images were used in a dignified manner, most being used to fulfill the ever increasing tourist market. By the year 1918 it is estimated that over five million cards of Fijian subject matter had been produced.

"Vanity," A Fijian Lass.

Published by Michelmore and printed in England, circa 1925. An unflattering, comic-like card of the period.

Typical Fijian Girls.

Bula *is a Fijian greeting or expression of good health.*

Card published by British and Foreign Imports, Milan Italy, circa 1910.

A. M. Brodziak & Co., Suva - Fiji

Fijian Maidens

A very early card published by A. Brodziak and Company Suva, circa 1899. Non-divided back.

Native Women Bathing, Fiji.   Harry Gardiner, Suva, Fiji.

Published by Harry Gardiner, Suva, circa 1917. Harry Gardiner had the distinction of being the first European child born on the small island of Mago, in 1873. He was an accomplished entrepreneur of the time period and by 1917 was well established as a "purveyor of postcards, curios, Vaseline Hair Tonic, shaving requisites, Fiji baskets and fans."

Fijians making Tappa cloth

Published by A. M. Brodziak & Co., Suva, Fiji.

Making Tappa, Fiji.

72375 J. W. Waters, Suva, Fiji. Copyright.

Published by A. M. Brodziak, Suva, circa 1910. Adolphus Meyer Brodziak was born in Sydney in the year 1850 and arrived in Levuka Fiji in 1870. With L. Cohen he began a partnership known as Cohen and Brodziak. In 1875 he bought out his partner and changed the name to A.M. Brodziak. His first postcards were produced in 1899 and ceased in 1911. The firm dealt in a wide variety of merchandise with offices located in Suva, Sydney, Nausori, Lbasa, and Navua. Among the items listed for sale in a 1914 advertisement were champagne, shoes, cement, and cigarettes. The firm closed its doors in 1933 and was acquired by Morris Hedstrom Ltd. In this card the women are in the final stages of beating tapa, or bark cloth.

A stunning early card published by J.W. Waters, Suva, circa 1900. In this card the art of painting tapa is pictured. Tapa, or barkcloth, was produced throughout Polynesia. It was manufactured by stripping and beating the bark of various native trees. In Fijian it is known as *masai,* and is still produced today. Non-divided back.

Fiji has a combined land mass of approximately 11,000 square miles. It is slightly smaller than New Jersey.

Real photo postcard marked "British made, Caine series, Suva," circa 1920. Frederick William Caine was born in Liverpool in 1870. By the time he reached Fiji in 1913 he had traveled the world as an experienced photographer and marksman of note. Financially secure, he took over the Le Faivre Art Studios and by 1915 changed the name to "The Caine Studios." His company was the first purveyors of Kodak cameras and photographic equipment in Fiji. The firm survives to this day as a photographic business in Suva and is currently owned by the family of one of Caine's later partners, the Jannif's.

Making Tappa Fiji 10

Entitled "Vicka Malolo - Fiji," this card produced in Australia depicts seated dancers. Publisher unknown, circa 1910.

VICKA MALOLO, FIJI.

Like many areas of the Pacific, the indigenous Fijian people were almost wiped out by raging epidemics in 1874.

"CO-OP COPYRIGHT"

Glamour Dance Girls, Fiji

3B238-N

Fijian Maiden

A. M. Brodziak & Co., Suva - Fiji

A very early card published by A. Brodziak and Company Suva, circa 1899. Here a woman of high rank is shown complete in all her finery. Non-divided back.

A rather late card marked "Co-Op Copyright." Publisher unknown, circa 1925.

Kava making in Fiji.

Entitled "Kava making in Fiji," this card by Gus Arnold, Suva, is circa 1907. The *Kava* tradition fascinated Westerners and was a popular subject matter.

UVEA. - Yagona, a drink prepared with a peppered root, which is chewed by native girls

A very early card, publisher unknown, circa 1899. A poignant view, probably taken from a much earlier photograph by one of the Dufty brothers in the early 1870s. The two brothers had one of the earliest photographic studios operating in Levuka beginning in 1871. Non-divided back.

FIJIAN MAIDENS MAKING KAVA.   [Published by Arnold and Co., Suva.

A typical *Kava* card of the period published by Arnold and Company, Suva, circa 1907.

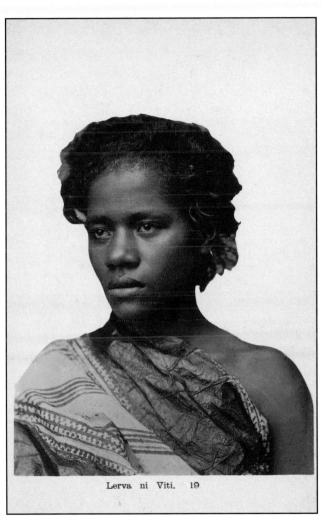

Entitled "Adi Cakaban - A favourite Princess of Fiji" this card produced in Australia is a portrait of Yadi Cakobau, grand-daughter of the great chief Cakobau and daughter of his second son, Ratu Timoce. She was a favorite subject for postcard portraits. Publisher unknown, circa 1910.

Very early card carrying a penciled in date on reverse of 1898, publisher unknown. Non-divided back.

Popular card published by Raphael Tuck and Sons Ltd., London, circa 1910. Part of the "South Seas Islanders Series" the inscription on the reverse is worth noting for prevailing views of the period. *"Fiji - types of beauty - Fiji Islands (South Pacific) discovered by Tasman in 1643. Under British Control since 1874. Soil very productive; climate hot, but agreeable. The native women are dark in colour and handsome, if somewhat muscular; clean and particular about their personal appearance, and passionately fond of flowers. The pottery made by these ladies is the best in the South Seas."*

Fijian Girl.

Very early card, publisher unknown, circa 1899. Non-divided back.

The rare Golden cowrie shell is found in Fiji and is considered sacred. Many local legends are attached to it.

A rare early card published by L.N. Anderson in Levuka 1904. Leslie Norman Anderson was a photographer of note and was active as a photographer and producer of postcards in Fiji from 1904 to possibly as late as 1936. The present postcard is his earliest datable card known, carrying the date of July 15, 1904. Non-divided back.

Three Maias from Lau (Fiji)

Presenting Yaqona, Fiji

3B228-N

GIRL IN TAPPA CLOTH. FIJI.   15

A rather late card marked "Co-Op Copyright," publisher unknown, circa 1925. In this scene a villager presents a cup of *Yagona* or *Kava* to the viewer.

Postcard marked "British made, Caine series, Suva," circa 1920. An interesting note was found attached to the card stating, *"This is one of my most popular cards F.W. Caine."*

P1. FIJIAN FISHER GIRL   COPYRIGHT

Entitled "Fijian Fisher Girl," circa
1920. Photographer unknown.

The two major exports from Fiji today are copra from which coconut oil is extracted and
"Fijian" water.

Real photo postcard, circa 1920.
Photographer unknown.

FIJIAN BELLES "ALL DRESSED UP" AT SUVA, FIJI ISLANDS. 1-61

Vale Levu or the chiefs "great house" always occupied the most prominent position in a Fijian village.

A GROUP OF CHIEF GIRLS, FIJI.

Popular card published by Raphael Tuck and Sons Ltd., London, circa 1910. Part pf the "South Sea Islanders Series" the inscription on the reverse is worth noting for the prevailing views of the period. "A Group of Chiefs Girls, Fiji - Fiji Islands, 225 in number, 80 inhabited, from a British Colony in the South Pacific. The natives are dark in colour, but some of them handsome. As the picture shows, most of the women have adopted European dress, though, strange to say, thousands have since died of pulmonary complaints, which previously were unknown. The houses are thatched, and well supplied with mats, fans, and cooking utensils."

23

Fiji is the only area in Polynesia to have an active gold mine.

Native Women, Fiji

A rather late card marked "Co-Op Copyright," publisher unknown, circa 1925.

DUSKY PSYCHES. [Published by Arnold and Co., Suva.

A sultry image entitled "Dusky Psyches" it was published by Arnold and Company, Suva, circa 1907. Gus Augustus Arnold moved from Sydney to Fiji and operated a tobacconist, hairdressing. and fancy goods business located next to the Pier Hotel in Suva. Although not a photographer he purchased rights from contemporary photographers, and not surprisingly his cards are often duplicated by other firms of the day. The company was sold in 1911 to employee Vivian Hargrave.

Bathing - Fiji

G. L. Griffiths, Suva, Fiji

Published by G.L. Griffiths, Suva, circa 1902. George Lyttleton Griffiths (1844-1908) founded the first newspaper in Fiji with his partner J.H. Hobson in 1869. By 1870 he was sole proprietor publishing his first cards in 1902. Born in London, he immigrated to New Zealand and then onto Fiji in 1869. Non-divided back.

Making Baskets, Fiji.

Published by J.W. Waters, Suva, circa 1900. John William Waters was one of the more interesting characters of the Pacific, having put to sea from London at the age of 16. By 1886, after a string of unusual and often hair raising occupations, he started a photography studio where he soon had great acclaim. Although his professional career as a photographer is hard to track down, he was by far the most prolific of the early photographers operating out of Fiji. Non-divided back.

Published by B. J. Boisse, Honolulu, circa 1907. A very rare and unusual card with the letters of "Aloha" spelled out in a montage of hula girls.

The first picture postcard appeared in Hawaii in December of 1897, before Hawaii became a U. S Territory in 1898. These early cards are quite rare and are termed "pioneer cards," being privately printed and mailed with a Kingdom of Hawaii stamp affixed. Used postal cards such as these can command from $1,000 to $3,000 in price. In thirty years of collecting, the author has come across only a handful of such cards, with 17 residing in his personal collection.

Very rare early pioneer card, publisher unknown, circa 1897. Entitled "Hawaiian Hula Dancers" the reverse of the card is marked "Hawaiian Postal Card." Non-divided back.

The Hawaiian Islands

Prior to March 1, 1907 the United States Post Office did not allow any message to be written on the back or address side of the card. Due to this the reverse side of the post-cards did not have "divided backs" but just had an area for the address. After this date came the "divided back" which allowed for both a short message and address to be written. Prior to 1907 only messages were seen on the image side of the postcard and were very brief in nature with the most notable penned quote of the time period being "wish you were here".

The Hawaiian Islands

The islands of Hawaii are the most remote in the world and consist of eight primary islands Niihau, Kauai, Oahu, Molokai, Lanai, Maui, Kahoolawe, and Hawaii. Like other areas in Polynesia, there are many schools of thought on the origins of the Hawaiian people. It is generally believed that the first migration originated from the Marquesas Islands, around 600AD, and a second migration from Tahiti at a later date.

Captain James Cook is credited for being the first non Polynesian to sight the islands in 1778, but in reality the Spanish, as far back as 1527, may have had contact with the islands. After Captain Cook's arrival and subsequent death in Hawaii, a long and steady stream of explorers, whalers, and traders visited the island group. Hawaiian culture greatly changed after these early contacts, but it was the arrival of the first missionaries from Boston, Massachusetts, in 1820, that undoubtedly had the largest impact. Many of the early missionaries became powerful business leaders, often inter-marrying with highborn Hawaiians, thus strengthening powerful alliances within the Hawaiian monarchy. In 1893 the last reigning monarch, Queen Lili'uokalani was overthrown by a group of American business men. Shortly afterwards, in 1898, the islands, long recognized for their strategic position in the Pacific, were annexed by the United States. During these years as a territory, Hawaii, and especially Waikiki, became a playground for the wealthy. Later, in 1959, Hawaii became a state and with the dawn of jet air travel the islands changed forever with the large increase in tourism.

Long fabled for the exoticness, like Tahiti the islands conjure up visions of an earthly paradise where life is free from everyday worries and where nature is defied with its profusion of vegetation, gentle rolling surf, volcanoes, and its native population. From the 18th century onward early writers and explorers filled their readers and armchair travelers with these visions adding to the islands romantic allure.

Filled with Aloha, the women were depicted as nymphs of sensuality which was an escape from the prevailing Victorian and Edwardian sensibilities of the day – it was this image and the distinctive beauty of the women that was translated into the postcards you see in the following pages. Even today these images are used to send the message of Aloha and exoticness throughout the world.

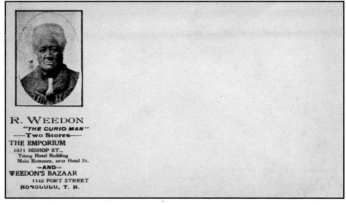
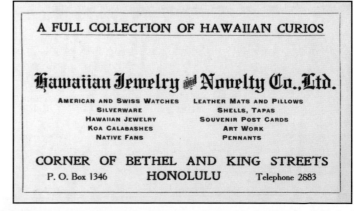

Very early card, publisher unknown, circa 1898. The reverse of the card is marked "Private Mailing Card - Authorized by Act of Congress, May 19, 1898." Non-divided back.

Very early card, publisher unknown, circa 1898. The reverse of the card is marked "Private Mailing Card - Authorized by Act of Congress, May 19, 1898." Non-divided back.

The original ancient Hawaiian Hula dancers wore skirts and wrappings of kapa, or barkcloth. In the 1870s, the legendary grass skirt was introduced into the islands by plantation workers from the Gilbert Islands.

4. Hawaiian Girl.

Rare early card published as part of the "Aloha Nui" series by the Art Lithography Company of San Francisco for the Island Curio Store, Honolulu, circa 1903. Non-divided back.

1 HAWAIIN GIRL

PUBLISHED BY THE ISLAND CURIO STORE, HONOLULU

Early card and the first card in the "Greetings From Hawaiian Island" series published by the Island Curio Store, Honolulu, circa 1903. Non-divided back.

NO. 2553. HAWAIIAN ISLANDS. A HAWAIIAN BEAUTY.
Published by Karl Lewis, Photographer, No. 136-D, Honmura Road, Yokohama

Rare early hand tinted card entitled "Hawaiian Islands - A Hawaiian Beauty" published by Karl Lewis Photographer, Yokohama Japan, circa 1900. Non-divided back.

70. Happy Hawaiian Girl.

64 HAWAIIAN TYPES

PUBLISHED BY THE ISLAND CURIO STORE HONOLULU

6. Hawaiian Belle.

Entitled "Happy Hawaiian Girl" this card was published by the Island Curio Company, James Steiner Honolulu, circa 1910.

Early card published as part of the "Aloha Nui" series by the Island Curio Store, Honolulu, circa 1903. Entitled "Hawaiian Types" card is printed on back "Private Mailing Card - Authorized by Act of Congress, May 18, 1898." Non-divided back.

Published as part of the "Aloha Nui" series by the Art Lithography Company of San Francisco for Wall Nichols Co. Ltd., Honolulu, circa 1902. Non-divided back.

1. HAWAIIAN GIRL

PUBLISHED BY THE ISLAND CURIO STORE HONOLULU.

62 HAWAIIAN GIRL

PUBLISHED BY THE ISLAND CURIO STORE HONOLULU

Early card and the first card of the "Aloha Nui" series published by the Island Curio Store, Honolulu, circa 1903. Entitled "Hawaiian Girl," card is printed on back "Private mailing card—Authorized by Act of Congress, May 18, 1898," Non-divided back.

Early card published as part of the "Aloha Nui" series by the Island Curio Store, Honolulu, circa 1903. Entitled "Hawaiian Girl" card is printed on back "Private Mailing Card - Authorized by Act of Congress, May 18, 1898." Non-divided back.

Early card published as part of the "Aloha Nui" series by the Island Curio Store, Honolulu, circa 1903. Entitled " Always Summer - Hawaii" card is printed on back "Private Mailing Card - Authorized by Act of Congress, May 18, 1898." Non-divided back.

Entitled "Hawaiian Islands Beauty" this card was published by the Island Curio Co., James Steiner Honolulu, circa 1910.

Early card published as part of the "Aloha Nui" series by the Island Curio Store, Honolulu, circa 1903. Entitled "Hawaiian Hula Dancer" card is printed on back "Private Mailing Card - Authorized by Act of Congress, May 18, 1898." Non-divided back.

Hawaii is the most isolated population center on the face of the earth, 2,390 miles from California; 3,850 miles from Japan; 4,950 miles from China; and 5,300 miles from the Philippines.

6 A HAWAIIAN BELLE

Early card published by the Hawaii and South Seas Curio Co., Honolulu, circa 1900. Entitled "A Hawaiian Belle" this beautiful young woman appears in numerous postcards and photographs of the time period. Non-divided back.

Entitled "Hawaiian Girls - Honolulu" this card was published in Germany as part of the "Aloha Nui" series by Hawaii and South Seas Curio Co., Honolulu, circa 1908.

Published in Germany for the Hawaii and South Seas Curio Co., Honolulu, circa 1908.

Entitled "Wela Ka Hao - My Honolulu Girl" this rare and early card was published in Germany as part of the "Aloha Nui" series by the Hawaii and South Seas Curio Co., Honolulu, circa 1900. This is the earliest known card to have a printed message in the native Hawaiian language other then just the word Aloha.

Hawaiian Beauty.

Entitled "Hawaiian Beauty" this card was published by the Wall Nichols Co. Ltd., Honolulu, circa 1908.

Entitled "Hawaiian Girl" this card was published by the Hawaii and South Seas Curio Co., Honolulu, circa 1910.

HAWAIIAN GIRL.

Hawaiian Lady, Honolulu.

Entitled "Hawaiian Lady - Honolulu" this card was published in Germany for the Hawaii and South Seas Curio Co., Honolulu, circa 1908.

223 CARNATION LEI, HAWAIIAN ISLANDS.

Entitled "Carnation Lei - Hawaiian Islands"
this card was published by the Island
Curio Company, Honolulu, circa 1907.

Hawaiian Beauties, Hawaiian Islands.

Entitled "Hawaiian Beauties - Hawaiian
Islands," circa 1907. Publisher unknown.

Early card published by the Hawaii and South Seas Curio Co., Honolulu, circa 1900. Published as part of the "Aloha Nui" series this card was extremely risqué at the time and in reality actually depicts women from Samoa, not Hawaii.

There are no racial or ethnic majorities in Hawaii; everyone is a minority. Caucasians (or Haoles) constitute about 34%, Japanese-Americans about 32%, Filipino-Americans about 16%, and Chinese-Americans about 5%. Hawaii is known as the melting pot of the Pacific, as it is very difficult to determine racial identification since most of the population has a mixture of ethnicities.

Entitled "A Hawaiian Belle – Hawaii" this card was published by the Hawaii and South Seas Curio Co., Honolulu, circa 1910.

Entitled "Hawaiian Style" this card was published by the Island Curio Company, Honolulu, circa 1907.

Entitled "Hula – Hula Dancer, Hawaiian Islands" this card was published by the Island Curio Company, James Steiner Honolulu, circa 1910.

Entitled "Hawaiian Schoolgirl" this card was published by the Island Curio Company, James Steiner Honolulu, circa 1910.

Aloha nui.

Honolulu
Oct 3rd

We are spending a few weeks here for Emma's health which is being benifited it is an ideal place for a vacation for a big man no cable and little chance for mail

Ernest

Hawaiian Belle.

Very rare early pioneer card, publisher unknown, circa 1898. Entitled "Hawaiian Belle" this card has a Kingdom of Hawaii stamp affixed as postage and is postmarked October 3, 1898. Non-divided back.

A HAWAIIAN BELLE.

Early and rare card published by the Hawaii and South Seas Curio Co., Honolulu, circa 1900. Entitled "A Hawaiian Belle" this is an unusual representation of a Hawaiian woman complete with a "Gibson Girl" hairstyle and dress. Non-divided back.

48B Hula-Hula Dancer - Hawaiian Islands.

Entitled "Hula - Hula Dancer - Hawaiian Islands" this card was published by the Island Curio Co., James Steiner Honolulu, circa 1910.

Scarce advertising card for Oceanic Steam Ship Company, circa 1910. Entitled "Pala - South Seas" the artwork is by O.G. Coutts.

Published by Wall Nichols and Company, Honolulu, circa 1900. Entitled "Hawaiian Beauty" this card is typical in its depiction of hula girls of the time period. Non-divided back.

Entitled "Hawaiian Belle" this card was published in Germany for the Hawaii and South Seas Curio Co, Honolulu, circa 1908.

Scarce advertising card for Oceanic Steam Ship Company, circa 1910. Entitled "Girl of Paradise, South Seas" this card is truly reminiscent of a painting by Paul Gauguin. Artwork by O.G. Coutts.

"Why the Ship was Wrecked"

Novelty card published by B.J. Boisse, Honolulu, circa 1907.

Novelty card published by Hawaii and South Seas Curio Co., Honolulu, circa 1915. Interesting printed inscription on reverse, "*The lure of the Hawaiian maid for the voyager in the Southern Seas has been the theme of writers from time long since; her exquisite beauty and charm of manner has oft times led him from the narrow path of duty.*"

Novelty card published by the Island Curio Co., James Steiner Honolulu, circa 1910. James Steiner was born in 1860 in Czechoslovakia and arrived in Honolulu in 1882 on a trip around the world. Finding employment with Hart and Company as a salesman he eventually became a partner and later owner in the 1890s. After seventeen years of hard work he began construction of his three-story "Elite" building in downtown Honolulu, complete with a popular ice cream parlor. This building was to be the home of Island Curio Store, which was a purveyor of souvenirs for the increasing tourist market. Among the many items sold were old Hawaiian stamps, calabashes, tapa cloth, poi pounders, canoe models and of course postcards. The first Island Curio Store postcards were produced in 1903. In 1907 the name was changed to the Island Curio Company. In 1914 the business was sold to Fred H. McNamarra, a business associate. It has been estimated that over a million postcards were produced by the firm in the years 1903 to 1914.

The Girls in These South Sea Islands Dress Mostly in Black I Saw a Great Deal of Them

Hand-colored real photo postcard by J.J. Williams, Honolulu, circa 1916.

Early hand tinted real photo postcard, circa 1907. Photographer unknown.
A unusual and rather sensual portrayal of a young Hawaiian girl.

Real photo postcard, circa 1915. Photographer unknown.

Real photo postcard, circa 1910. Photographer unknown.

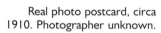

Real photo postcard, circa 1915. Photographer unknown.

Real photo postcard, circa 1905. Photographer unknown. Non-divided back.

Real photo postcard, circa 1905. An unusually risqué card for the time period. Photographer unknown. Non-divided back.

Real photo postcard, circa 1905. An unusually risqué card for the time period. Non-divided back.

Real photo postcard, circa 1905. An unusually risqué card for the time period. Photographer unknown. Non-divided back.

Real photo postcard, circa 1905. Photographer unknown. Non-divided back.

Real photo postcard, circa 1910. Photographer unknown.

Real photo postcard, circa 1905. Photographer unknown. Non-divided back.

Real photo postcard, circa 1905. An unusually risqué card for the time period. Photographer unknown. Non-divided back.

Real photo postcard, circa 1905. An unusually risqué card for the time period. Photographer unknown. Non-divided back.

Real photo postcard by J.J. Williams, Honolulu, circa 1916. J.J. Williams was one of Honolulu's most popular and largest photographic portrait galleries. In 1882 he began by purchasing the photography business of Menzies Dickson. The earliest promoter of tourism in the islands, he established the famous *Paradise of the Pacific* journal that would later be published until the 1960s in magazine format. This periodical was entirely devoted to Hawaiian tourist travel and island life. Like many photographers and galleries of the day, he combined curios with island views and postcards to supply the ever-increasing tourist market.

Mauna Kea is the tallest mountain in the world, when measured from the base of the ocean floor.

Real photo postcard, circa 1915. Photographer unknown.

Real photo postcard entitled " A maid of old Hawaii," by Ray Jerome Baker, Honolulu, circa 1915. Born in Rockford Illinois, Ray Jerome Baker (1880-1972) without a doubt became one of Hawaii's most prolific photographers. Arriving in Honolulu on a two week vacation with his wife, he took dozens of photographs while touring the islands. So stricken with the natural beauty and the people he later returned in 1910 to permanently settle and open a photographic studio in Honolulu. He had a long career as a photographer and lecturer including having traveled to more then sixty countries by the 1920s. He was also a motion picture cameraman of note, having worked for Pathe News Agency. He took the only motion pictures of the funeral of Queen Liliuokalani in 1917. Today his photographs and postcards are eagerly sought by collectors worldwide.

Real photo postcard entitled "Along the shore of Molokai" by Ray Jerome Baker, Honolulu, circa 1915.

Kilauea, on the island of Hawaii, is the world's most active volcano.

Real photo postcard, circa 1915.
Photographer unknown.

Real photo postcard by J.J. Williams,
Honolulu, circa 1915.

Real photo postcard, circa 1915. Photographer unknown.

Iolani Palace is the only royal palace in the United States.

Real photo postcard, circa 1905. Photographer unknown. Non-divided back.

Real photo postcard, circa 1915. Photographer unknown.

The Hawaiian Islands are the projecting tops of the biggest mountain range in the world.

Real photo postcard by J.J. Williams, Honolulu, circa 1916.

Real photo postcard, circa 1915. Photographer unknown.

Real photo postcard by Wofford, circa 1944.

Real photo postcard, circa 1915. Photographer unknown.

Real photo postcard, circa 1905. Photographer unknown. Non-divided back.

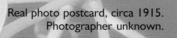

Real photo postcard, circa 1915.
Photographer unknown.

Entitled "Hawaiian Girl" this card was published by the Mid Pacific Curio Store, Honolulu, circa 1920. Printed inscription on reverse *"The famous flower girls of Hawaii can be seen on all street corners and in the markets of Hawaii and other places on the island where they vend their perfumed pua or roses, each one being decorated with a beautiful wreath or lei around her neck. Hawaii is famed for its profusion of beautiful flowers and it is the native custom to cover travelers when they arrive or depart with the beautiful flower leis."*

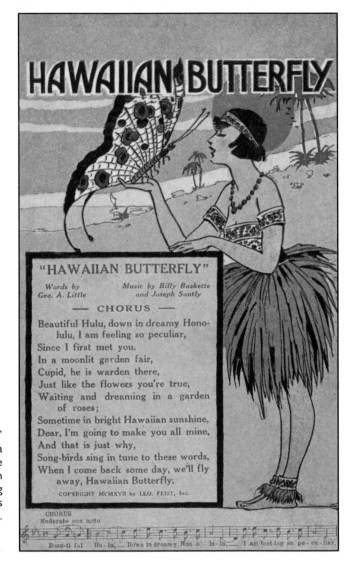

Rare sheet music card for "Hawaiian Butterfly," published by Leon Feist Inc., circa 1923. On this card a "flapper" hula girl of the 1920s is depicted. A massive amount of Hawaiian sheet music was published from the 1870s through the 1930s to fill the ever increasing demand. By the 1920s, Hawaiian music had found its way into mainstream American culture.

Some famous Hollywood Hula Girls appeared in popular movies, including: Clara Bow in "Hula" 1927, Jeanette MacDonald in "Lets Go Native" 1930, Minnie Mouse In "Hawaiian Holiday" 1935, Dorothy Lamour in "Road to Singapore" 1940, Betty Grable in "Song of the Islands" 1942, Rita Hayworth in "Sadie Thompson" 1954, and Marjorie Mann in "Ma and Pa Kettle at Waikiki" 1955.

Real photo postcard, circa 1915. Photographer unknown.

Real photo postcard, circa 1920.
Photographer unknown.

Real photo postcard, circa 1915. Photographer unknown.

The Big Island is Hawaii's largest, at 4,038 square miles. It is twice the size of all other Hawaiian Islands combined.

Real photo postcard, circa 1915.
Photographer unknown.

> *The wettest spot on earth is on the island of Kauai, on Mount Wai'ale'ale. It has recorded as much as 600 inches of rain in one year.*

Real photo postcard, circa 1915. Photographer unknown.

Published by Alta Printing Co.,
San Francisco, circa 1925.

Real photo postcard, circa 1945.
Photographer unknown.

Real photo postcard, circa 1915. Photographer unknown.

Real photo postcard, circa 1915. Photographer unknown. Interesting inscription on reverse of card " *She can sure shake it up.*"

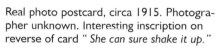

Real photo postcard, circa 1915. Photographer unknown.

Real photo postcard, circa 1915. Photographer unknown.

153 Hula Girl, Hawaiian Islands

The largest contiguous ranch in the United States is in Hawaii. The Parker Ranch, near Kamuela, has about 480,000 acres of land.

Real photo postcard, circa 1930. Photographer unknown.

Real photo postcard, circa 1915. Photographer unknown.

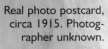

Fisher maidens at Kailua Beach - Is. Oahu - Hawaii

Real photo postcard entitled "Fisher maidens at Kailua Beach - Is. Oahu - Hawaii" by the Nielen Co., Cinncinnati, circa 1936.

Novelty card, publisher unknown, circa 1940. Printed instructions on reverse *"Keep this tab in three inches of water at all times. Do not place in direct sunlight - Sprouts in 4 to 7 days. Grows for 2 or 3 weeks."*

Rare novelty card published by N.E.Y.R.P. in Madrid Spain, circa 1940. This card is done with the application of silk thread to the skirt and leis.

Novelty card published by Kahuna Komics, Honolulu, circa 1942. A popular comic card published during World War Two for the military market. Artwork by Ted Mundorff. Born in Pittsburgh, Mundorff attended Punahou School in Honolulu. After graduating he left the islands and returned in 1936 and established an artist's studio under the name of the "Hawaiian Pallet" in downtown Honolulu. Most famous for his illustrations of Hawaiian flowers, he was also an accomplished cartoonist having a weekly series in the 1950s under the name of "Walter Winchell's Hawaii."

Novelty card, publisher unknown, circa 1940. Art work by Ted Mundorff.

Real photo postcard, circa 1925. Photographer unknown.
A unusual burlesque type image of the time period.

The island of Oahu, with Honolulu as the state's capital, draws more visitors than any other island in Hawaii. One-third of the state's best surfing beaches are on Oahu.

Real photo postcard, circa 1915. Photographer unknown.

A popular card of the period featuring three Maori women. Photographs by Frank Denton, Wanganui. Marked "F.T. series and published by Wilson and Company, Auckland," circa 1910.

The combined land area of New Zealand is 268,680 square miles, about the size of Wyoming.

Chapter 4

New Zealand

New Zealand, or *Aotearoa*, Land of the Long White Cloud, is an isolated group of two islands laying 1200 miles southeast of Australia and a similar distance south-south-west of Tonga. The two islands are mountainous, especially the South Island, where the Southern Alps rise 12,000 feet. The North Island has a vast area of rich lowlands, where the early Polynesian Maori settled the rich fertile coastal areas around 1,000 A.D. The first wave of migration originated from Tahiti and later from the Marqueas, with oral traditions placing a much earlier date on these migrations.

The first European visitor to this land was Dutch explorer Abel Tasman, who sighted the islands in 1642 and lost four of his men in a brief skirmish with the fierce Maori inhabitants. There was no further contact until Captain James Cook arrived in Poverty Bay in October of 1769. This was one of Cook's many stops in the islands over the next several years. Similar to other areas in Polynesia, missionaries soon arrived in the first quarter of the 19th century, with the Church Missionary Society of London exerting the most influence.

In 1840 the Maori chiefs entered into a compact with Great Britain called "The Treaty of Waitangi," in which they ceded sovereignty to Queen Victoria while retaining territorial rights. In that same year, the British began the first organized colonial settlement. Shortly after, a series of land wars developed between 1843 and 1872, ending with the defeat of the native Maori peoples. Later, in 1907, the British colony of New Zealand became an independent Dominion that supported the United Kingdom militarily in both World Wars. Today, New Zealand is currently addressing and struggling with the long-standing Maori grievances. Standing in the forefront of "Green" nations, the leading sources of income today are tourism, timber, agriculture, meat, dairy products, and banking.

New Zealand was, without a doubt, the largest producer of picture postcards in Polynesia. It has been estimated that between 1909 and 1915, at the height of the picture postcard craze, 10 to 15 million postcards were posted in the Dominion. World Fairs and International Expositions also prompted the production of picture postcards in New Zealand, with numerous photographers and publishers operating throughout the country as well as in Great Britain and Germany.

A rare card published by the Tanner Brothers in Auckland and marked on reverse "Pocket Novelty Card," circa 1910. Under the image of the Maori woman is an accordion fold out of Auckland and vicinity.

"Maori Girls - Dark, but Comely" photograph by James Iles, of Rotorua, and published as part of the S and M series - possibly for the firm of Valentine and Sons, Dundee Scotland, circa 1900. The title of this card gives the present day viewer a look into the racism that was prevalent at the turn of the 20th century. Non-divided back.

No. 56 Meditation.

"Maori Girl, Rotorua" published as part of the F.T. series. Photographer unknown, circa 1900. Non-divided back.

Maori Girl, Rotorua. N. Z.

"Meditation" publisher and photographer unknown, circa 1910. Esoteric titles such as this were popular with photographers and painters of the time period.

The total population of New Zealand is just under 4 million inhabitants, with nearly one in ten being of Maori descent.

Real photo postcard and issued as part of the "Tanner Brothers Photographic Series," photograph by Frank Denton of Wanganui, circa 1915. One of the photographers favorite models is depicted here wearing a traditional kiwi feather cloak.

Maori Woman wearing Kiwi Mat, N.Z.

Real photo postcard entitled "Maori Beauty" and issued as part of the Tanner Brothers Maoriland Photographic Series," photograph by Frank Denton of Wanganui, circa 1915. This is by far one of the most popular real photo postcards of the time period, and was reproduced numerous times in various books and publications.

Maori Beauty, N.Z.

Under the Fern

Iles, Photo.   S. M. & Co.'s Series

An enticing image entitled "Under the Fern." From an original photo by James Isles for the S & M Co. series, circa 1900. James Isles operated a thriving photographic studio at Oamaru in Rotorua from 1878 to the late 1920s. He was well known, like fellow photographer Frank Denton, for his "Maori Beauties." Non-divided back.

Ferns played a very important part in Maori life, with the bracken root being a staple food as well as being used for building and fencing. The fern could sometimes be a verbal symbol of chieftainship in the Maori language. At least 45 kinds of spirals are used in Maori carving and tattoo are thought to have originated from the fern.

MAORI WOMAN, TAUERU.   F.T. Series, No. 2182.

Photo. by Winzenberg.

"Maori Woman, Taueru," photographed by Winzenberg. Published as part of the "F.T. series" in Great Britain for Valentine and Sons, Dundee, Scotland, circa 1910.

129. Maori Girl

Muir & Moodie

"Maori Girl" published by the firm of Muir and Moodie, Dunedin, circa 1902. Non-divided back. A beautiful image with the young woman dressed in a traditional kiwi feather cloak and *hei tiki* around her neck.

A MAORI WAHINE.

"A Maori Wahine," published by the H.B. card company of Great Britain, circa 1915. In this seductive view the model is seen posing dressed in a flax cloak, jade *mere* in hand.

The art of tattoo is still widely practiced by the Maori. The word for tattoo in Maori is "moko."

A *mere* is a short, flat weapon made of jade or greenstone. Highly treasured and containing much mana, they were used in hand-to-hand combat. The mana *represented great ancestral authority.*

Maori Beauty.

A card published as part of the "F/T/ series" by the firm of Valentine and Sons, Dundee, Scotland, circa 1910. In this photo, the young woman is holding a *patu paraoa,* possibly indicating she is the oldest in the family.

In the 18th century, distinctive pounamu, or greenstone, ornaments were greatly admired by the Maori. The most distinctive and highly regarded ornament was the hei tiki, a carved greenstone figure with tilted head. The exact meaning of these ornaments remains unclear, some consider them to be a sign of fertility while others believe them to be representations of tiki, the first man created by the Maori god Tane. These ornaments were worn by both men and women of rank and were passed down from one generation to another, accumulating more mana in the process.

"Pretty Young Maori Girl," published by T. Pringle, Wellington, circa 1908.

A card that was printed in Saxony for the Universal Postcard Company, circa 1910.

"Maoriland" postcard published by the Tanner Brothers with offices in Auckland, Wellington, and London, circa 1910.

"The Belle of New Zealand." Here the young woman is shown wearing a traditional flax cloak. Published by Muir and Moodie, Dunedin, circa 1902. The firm of Muir and Moodie was established in the year 1898, when Thomas Muir joined George Moodie upon the retirement of Alfred Burton. Many of the photographs used in the firm's postcards date to an earlier date, when Thomas Muir was in partnership with Alfred Burton. The firm of Muir and Moodie was in business until 1916. Non-divided back.

"Maori Girls." published by M and M, circa 1900. This type of image was extremely popular. Similar poses were used by most of the photographers of the day.

"Maori Beauty" published by the firm of Muir and Moodie, Dundedin circa 1902. Non-divided back.

74

Tatooed Maori Woman with Tiki (Maori God).

Maori women's tattoos, or moko, were limited to the lips and chins and are still popular today.

"Tattooed Maori Woman with Tiki (Maori God)," published by Wildman and Areys, circa 1910. A photo showing the traditional *hei tiki*, along with a chin and lip *moko* typical of the time period and done with the use of darning needles.

A MAORI MAIDEN.

A card that was printed in Saxony for the Universal Postcard Company, circa 1910. This same image appears in several Hawaiian versions as well, even though the young woman is clearly Maori.

New Zealand has two official languages, Maori and English.

Denton, Photo. *Maori Beauties* S. M. & Co.'s Series

"Maori Beauties," photograph by Frank Denton, Wanganui. Published by Valentine and Sons, Dundee, Scotland, S & M Co. series, circa 1900. Frank Denton (1869-1963) was important as both a commercial photographer and as a recorder of the many changes happening in the country at the time. Today, he is regarded for his artistic practice, which pushed the boundaries of the medium. Besides landscapes, he had a passion for the Maori people, which is evident today through his many photographs. Non-divided back.

Maori Wahine Mata, N.Z.

A card printed in Great Britain for the firm of Valentine and Sons, Dundee, Scotland, circa 1910. The photo for this card is most likely from an earlier image by James Isles of Rotorua. In this image, a classic piece of Maori architectural carving is seen in the background.

"VERY GOOD TE WHAKAHUA" (THE PHOTOGRAPH)

"Very Good *Te Whakahua*," published by T. Pringle, Wellington, circa 1908.

AN ARAWA GIRL

"An Arawa Girl," published by T. Pringle, Wellington, circa 1908.

Maori Girl (showing Tiki).

Dear Daisy
"*Many happy returns of the day.*" *from all. Mother will write later. Yours etc Arthur*

128

A Maori girl wearing a traditional *hei tiki* and parrot feather cloak, photographer and publisher unknown circa 1900. Non-divided back.

Maori Canoeist   Photo by Denton

c/o Tip Top Teas   Masterton N.Z.
2. 12. '03

We are writing a general letter to Weston. wh. no doubt will be passed on, but this is to wish you all every good wish for the New Year, and trust your dear Mother will soon be quite strong & well. We have been told what a great help & blessing you are to her & the rest of the family & feel sure you are glad you can assist so much. I have not attained the proportions of the lady on this card. but am better than I was & your uncle is very well & brown. He joins in fond love to your Father Mother Self & Boys. The latter I fear are growing apace — Good bye dear Winnifred   Yrs lovingly

"Maori Canoeist" photograph by Frank Denton, Wanganui. Published as part of the S and M series - possibly for the firm of Valentine and Sons, Dundee Scotland circa 1900. Non-divided back.

New Zealand is a land of active and dormant volcanoes, resulting in numerous earth-quakes.

Ani, the Village Belle

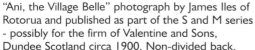

"Ani, the Village Belle" photograph by James Iles of
Rotorua and published as part of the S and M series
- possibly for the firm of Valentine and Sons,
Dundee Scotland circa 1900. Non-divided back.

A Maori Beauty

"A Maori Beauty" publisher and photographer
unknown circa 1900. Non-divided

Maori Beauty   F. T. Series. No. 634.

"Maori Beauty" published as part of the F.T.
series, photographer unknown circa 1910. Here
the Maori woman is sitting in a provocative pose
with her large greenstone *mere* in her lap. Her
moko or tattoo appears to have been done with
the use of darning needles which was a popular
way of applying chin tattoos at this time period.

MUSCULOSINE BYLA   XX. Polynesie

MAORI MAIDEN

Early French advertising trade card for "Musculosine Byla," circa 1890.

"Maori Maiden" published as part of the F.T. series from a photograph by Frank Denton circa 1910.

"KIA-ORA" Greetings from Maoriland.

Photo by Argent Archer, Kensington.

Popular card published by Argent Archer, Kensington. Published in Great Britian circa 1915.

Maori
Be les

Hongi *was a type of Maori greeting where both parties touched noses.*

"Maori Belles" photographer and publisher unknown circa 1900. Non divided back.

n Maori-
—and—
Under
e
Ferns

A rather exotic view showing two women in a fern forest, photographer and publisher unknown circa 1900. Non-divided back.

"The Arawa Belle," one of the more popular cards published by T. Pringle, Wellington, circa 1908.

You're far away
across the Sea,
So take this greeting
kind from me.
To wish you Health,
and all Good Cheer,
And Luck attend you
thro' the Year.

An unusual embossed "Heartiest Greeting" card published by the Tanner Brothers of Wellington, circa 1915.

Maori Beauty

PHILCO SERIES   7108 B

"Maori Beauty," embossed card published by the Philco Publishing Company, London. Photographer unknown, circa 1910. Embossed postcards like this were mainly produced with holiday greetings - Maori ones such as this are quite scarce, due to their high production price.

No. 82. Sadness

V. F.

A card entitled "Sadness" publisher and photographer unknown circa 1900. At the time this card was published there was a general feeling that the Maori people were a dying race. Two of New Zealand's most celebrated artists of this time period, Goldie and Lindauer, often painted portraits of the Maori people showing them in the same state of sadness, melancholy and despair. Non-divided back.

"A Maori Princess," publisher and photographer unknown, circa 1900. Non-divided back.

A Maori Princess

From Maoriland

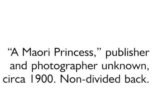

Early card from a photograph by Joseph Martin of Auckland. Published as part of the S and M series - possibly for the firm of Valentine and Sons, Dundee Scotland circa 1900. Joseph Martin (1843-1916) was one of New Zealands earliest photographic pioneers. Besides being a teacher and headmaster he was responsible for improving "instantaneous" photography using new a new gelatin bromide process discovered while touring London and visiting the Royal College of Chemistry in 1879. He formed a partnership with W.H.T. Partington and opened a studio in Auckland employing the new dry plate process. He gained an international reputation for his ethnographical and topographical photography after it was exhibited at various expositions in London and Paris. Non-divided back.

84

Group Maori Girls.   Muir & Moodie· 3178

An interesting view of a group of Maori women dressed in various types of traditional clothing.
Published by the firm of Miuir and Moodie, Dunedin, circa 1902. Non-divided back.

Maori Beauty. No. 10   Denton, Photo

"Maori Beauty," published and photographed by Frank Denton of Wanganui, circa 1900. Non-divided back.

A Maori Maid. Rotorua.   Iles, Photo.

"A Maori Maid," published and photographed by James Isles of Rotorua, circa 1900. Non-divided back.

"Maori Belles - Bay of Islands," published as part of the "F.T. series," photographer unknown, circa 1910. An interesting view showing the young women wearing flax garments placed over western clothing.

Maori Belles, Bay of Islands, N. Z.   F. T. Series. No. 545

Half-Cast Maori Girl. 350.   Tanner Bros.Ltd.

Real photo postcard entitled, "Half-Cast Maori Girl," published by the Tanner Brothers of Auckland, Wellington, and London, circa 1910. A rather racist card of the time period showing a mixed-race woman in an almost comical pose, complete with an old Maori carving in her hand.

Pounamu *is the Maori word for greenstone, or jade, that remains a very treasured material found on the South Island.*

Real photo postcard by Frank Denton, Wanganui, circa 1905. These two women depicted as "Maori Beauties" were some of the photographer's favorite models, appearing in numerous cards and photos of the time. Non-divided back.

Real photo postcard by Frank Duncan and Company, Auckland, circa 1910.

Real photo postcard by Frank Denton, Wanganui, circa 1910.

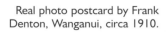

A Maori Maiden. F.G.R. 3377.

Real photo postcard by Frank Duncan and Company, Auckland, circa 1910. In this image the sitter is depicted wearing a fine flax cloak with ornate *taniko* border.

"Maori Girls - Bay of Islands," published as part of the "F.T. series," photographer unknown, circa 1910.

A card typical of the time period and published in Germany, publisher unknown, circa 1915. Both women in this image are depicted with chin tattoos, or *moko*.

Real photo postcard, photographer unknown, circa 1905. In this photo, four popular tourist guides at Rotorua are depicted and dressed in Maori finery. Non-divided back.

Real photo postcard entitled, "Maori Maidens," by Frank Duncan and Company of Auckland, circa 1915.

Rotorua has long been a popular tourist destination on the North Island, due to its thermal activity and Maori villages. No trip to New Zealand is complete without the obligatory visit.

Card published as part of the "F.T. series" and printed in England, photograph by Frank Denton of Wanganui, circa 1915.

Card published as part of the F.T. series and printed in England, photograph by Armstrong circa 1915.

Real photo postcard by Frank Duncan and Company, Auckland, circa 1910.

Mana *was a term used by the Maori and other peoples in Polynesia to express a supernatural or divine power. Objects as well as people could be instilled with mana, and therefore great care was taken with sacred objects and ruling Chiefs to protect them from having their power defiled.*

1018   A MAORI BEAUTY, N.Z.   (PROTECTED.)

A sultry card of the time period, publisher and photographer unknown, circa 1910.

Real photo postcard, publisher and photographer unknown, circa 1915. Marked on back "Industria - Series."

Real photo postcard by Frank Duncan and Company, Auckland, circa 1905. Entitled "A Maori Maiden," this beautiful image depicts a high-ranking, young woman dressed in a fine parrot feather cloak. Non-divided back.

Real photo postcard by Frank Duncan and Company, Auckland, circa 1905. Non-divided back.

Real photo postcard by Radcliffe, Wanganui, circa 1910. In this photo the young woman is holding a traditional *taiaha* in her hand.

501.

Guide Hara Whakarewarewa   E. Le Grice Photo.

"Guide Hara Whakarewarewa," published and photographed by E. Le Grice, Rotorua, circa 1910. Jeremiah Le Grice (1847-1919) had a photographic studio and general curio shop in the popular tourist destination of Rotorua, where tourists were led through Maori villages and thermal areas by guides, such as the one depicted on this card. Here the guide is dressed in her finery, complete with *taiaha* and large *hei tiki*.

The taiaha *is a two-handed weapon. The pointed, or carved, end was used to poke the opponent and then, when the moment was right, the taiaha would be reversed and the blade used to crack the opponent's skull. It was held in both hands and used to strike and parry blows. The Maori were highly skilled with this weapon.*

Real photo postcard issued as part of the "Tanner Brothers Maoriland Photographic Series," photograph by Frank Denton of Wanaganui, circa 1915.

Card published as part of the "F.T. series" and printed in England, photographer unknown, circa 1915. Marked "Plate Sunk Series" on reverse.

F.G.R.1961.
F.J.Denton.Wanoanui. Photo.

Real photo postcard by Frank Denton, Wanganui circa 1905. Non-divided back.

Samoa

Samoans are known throughout Polynesia as the "happy" people because of their good-natured, fun-loving spirit. Famous author Robert Louis Stevenson, after cruising throughout much of Polynesia, settled in Samoa. He is known in Samoa as Tusitalia, or "Teller of Tales." He fell in love with the people and the islands, and died there in 1894. He is buried at the top of Mt. Vaea.

Holst's Garten
(Inh.: Herm. Boedemann)
Braunschweig.

September 15th 97

Regards from
John Thuleao
Samoan Chief

Samoaner-Truppe.

Lichtdruck v. C. F. FAY, Frankfurt a. M.

Rare early pioneer card published by the firm of C.F. Fay, Frankfurt, circa 1897. A lovely depiction of a Samoan dancer that was postally used in Germany by a traveling dance troupe on Sept 16, 1897. Non-divided back.

TALOFA SAMOA

"Ausstellung Samoa"
Unsere neuen Landsleute

APIA.

Saw the Samoa's at the zoologischer-garten in Berlin July the 9th 1900.

Early German card published by the firm Giesecke and Devrient, Leipzig and Berlin, circa 1900. A romantic landscape with Apia harbor in the foreground and a young Samoan women used in a cameo format. Non-divided back.

Chapter 5

Samoa

The Islands of Samoa form a chain that lays approximately 1,200 miles from Tahiti and 300 miles from Tonga. Today, the islands are comprised of American Samoa, a U.S. trust territory, and Western Samoa, an independent country. The main islands in Western Samoa are Savai'i and in American Samoa, Upolu, and Tutuila. All of the islands, like Hawaii, are volcanic in origin, except small Rose Island, which is actually an atoll in the American group. On the island of Savai'i, volcanic slopes rise to over 6,000 feet with austere, dramatic scenery, while most of the other islands are wrapped in lush vegetation, rain forests, and crystal-clear lagoons.

There has been a long legacy of foreign intervention in the islands, after the first arrival of missionaries in 1830. Due to the islands' strategic location in the Pacific, they have been used as coaling stations and stopping-off points for merchants. The United States, Germany, and Great Britain intervened in local politics and disputes, including some among themselves, leading to the group being divided into two parts in 1889. The part administered by Germany was comprised of present-day Western Samoa, while the United States administered the eastern islands from Pago Pago, on Tutuila in American Samoa. In 1914, with the start of World War One, New Zealand occupied Western Samoa with their expeditionary forces. In 1920, under a mandate from the League of Nations, the islands continued under New Zealand's control until 1962, when they gained full independence.

Because of these colonial interests there was a multitude of cards printed in all four of the countries involved as well as in Samoa to provide for an ever-growing colonial presence. Hence, most of the early views were sent home by officers, sailors, and other visitors leading to a profusion of exotic voyeuristic themes, many with suggestive sexual overtones. Cards depicted not only the famous *kava* ceremony but also one of the more unusual aspects of Samoan society - the honoring of a virgin in each village. Titled, these young females known as *taupou* were usually the niece or daughter of a village chief. Holding the second highest position in the village the young women's duties were mainly ceremonial. Described by the noted anthropologist Margaret Mead as "the female ornament of the chiefs rank," they were depicted in early cards dressed in ornate costumes, as is seen in some of the views on the following pages.

Card by an unknown publisher, circa 1907.

A card depicting a young Samoan girl. This image was probably originally taken by photographer Thomas Andrew and appropriated by Theodor Eisman of Leipzig who then made it into his E.L. series and was then published by Ali Mohamed Fazal of Bombay, India, circa 1907.

No. J. SAMOA. The Head-maiden of a Samoan village.
Published by Karl Lewis, Photographer, No. 102, Honmura Road, Yokohama.

Samoan Girls

Four mailed this day 29/2/04

G. L. Griffiths. Suva. Fiji

This reclining view of Samoan girls published by G.L. Griffiths in Suva Fiji was quite provocative in its day. George Lyttleton Griffiths (1944-1908) was an important figure in the history of Fiji as it was Griffiths who founded the first newspaper in Fiji, with his partner J.H. Hobson in 1869. By 1870 he was sole proprietor publishing his first cards in 1902. Born in London, he immigrated to New Zealand and then onto Fiji in 1869. This card was mailed Feb 29, 1904. Non-divided back.

Titled "The head maiden of a Samoan village" hand-tinted, this image depicts a *taupou* complete with all her finery. Published by Karl Lewis Photographer, Yokohama, Japan, circa 1900. Non-divided back.

Greetings

Costumes d'apparat Samoa. Pago. Pago.

Two young Samoan women, most likely *taupou*. Published by A.J. Tattersall, Apia, circa 1910.

Tattoos, or pe'a demonstrate the strong ties that Samoans have to their culture. Samoans have practiced the art of tattooing men and women for over 2,000 years. On men, most tattoos cover the mid-back, down the sides, and the flanks to the knees. A woman's tattoo is not quite as extensive or heavy. The geometric designs are based upon ancient patterns and are associated with rank and status.

Samoan woman

Published by A. M. Brodziak & Co., Suva, Fiji.

"Samoan woman," published in Suva Fiji by A.M. Brodziak, circa 1910. Adolphus Meyer Brodziak was born in Sydney in the year 1850 and arrived in Levuka Fiji in 1870. With L. Cohen he began a partnership known as Cohen and Brodziak. In 1875 he bought out his partner and changed the name to A.M. Brodziak. His first postcards were produced in 1899 and ended in 1911. The firm dealt in a wide variety of merchandise with offices located in Suva, Sydney, Nausori, Lbasa, and Navua. Among the items listed for sale in a 1914 advertisement were champagne, shoes, cement, and cigarettes. The firm closed its doors in 1933 and was acquired by Morris Hedstrom Ltd.

Studio portrait published by Thomas Andrew, Apia, circa 1907.

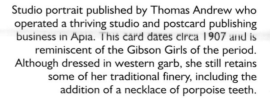

No. G. A Samoan school-teacher at T___lla. Published by Karl Lewis, Photographer, No. 102, Honm___ Road, Yokohama.

Unusual depiction of a school teacher, circa 1900. Published by Karl Lewis, Yokohama, Japan. Hand-tinted. Non-divided back.

Published by Thomas Andrew, Apia with printed inscription 1905.

Published by Thomas Andrew, Apia, with printed inscription 1905. Non-divided back.

Studio portrait published by Thomas Andrew who operated a thriving studio and postcard publishing business in Apia. This card dates circa 1907 and is reminiscent of the Gibson Girls of the period. Although dressed in western garb, she still retains some of her traditional finery, including the addition of a necklace of porpoise teeth.

SAMOAN GIRLS

Very visual and exotic image of three Samoan girls wearing traditional split whale tooth necklaces. Published by A.M. Brodziak in Suva, Fiji, circa 1907.

A young girl, possibly a *taupou*, dressed as a warrior with a sharp-bladed metal fighting knife. Originally introduced throughout the Pacific Islands to cut sugar cane, the knife was later appropriated by Samoans as a type of war club and later used in the "fire dance," which was a popular export to the West in the 1920s. "Published in Saxony, Germany" with no publishers name, it is marked "E.L. series," making it the possible production of Theodor Eisman, of Leipzig.

Samoan Woman published by Theodor Eismann, of Lepzig, circa 1907. This color lithographic card is part of the E.L. series with the word postcard printed in ten languages on the reverse making it saleable world-wide. Eismann was the first postcard manufacturer to come up with this revolutionary idea in marketing which was soon copied by other publishers of the day.

Unusual card with a dancer in a studio setting, circa 1910. Published in Apia by Alfred John Tattersall (1861-1951). Tattersall was the most prolific of photographers working in Apia. A New Zealander by birth he moved to the islands in 1886 to work for the already established portrait photographer John Davis. Upon Davis's death in 1893, Tattersall acquired all of his negatives. This combined with his own work led to a profusion of souvenir photos and postcards as well as the odd commission work.

Topless views like this were popular with the officers and sailors stationed or traveling through the islands. Published as part of the E.L. series by Theodor Eismann of Leipzig, circa 1907.

Siva Siva Dancer.

Samoan *Siva Siva* dancer published by the Hawaii and South Seas Curio Co. Honolulu, circa 1915. The printed inscription on the reverse added drama and saleability to both sender and recipient alike. "*The Royal Hula-hula dancing girls were a feature of olden days in Hawaii. The Hula-hula is acting out by gestures and movements the ideas expressed by the song which accompany them. The time is marked by striking on gourds of hokeo and in some instances these dancers are in honor of the Gods or chief as the alaapa-apa. The professional hula dancers are dvotees of the Goddess Laka. The dancers are generally women, though children are sometimes involved in the less objectionable dances and men act as buffoons between the acts. The Siva Siva is a similar dance of the South Seas.*"

Girl looking from Screen-Fiji (Samoan).

72364   J. W. Waters, Suva, Fiji. Copyright.

Early card with a backdrop of traditional Samoan and Fijian *tapa,* or barkcloth. Published by the firm of J.W. Waters, Suva Fiji, circa 1900. John William Waters originally put to sea from London at the age of 16. Non-divided back.

22706—SOUTH SEA, *Siva-Siva Dancing Girl.*

Popular depiction of a Samoan *Siva Siva* dancing girl, this image was published by the Souvenir Post Card Company of New York and was printed in Germany, circa 1910. This startling image shows the young studio sitter in fanciful native garb complete with hand-woven fans and tapa of the period.

Finely woven mats were exchanged in Samoa. The more mats a chief possessed and displayed, the richer he was. Such mats are still important as a method of paying tribute at weddings, funerals, and other public events.

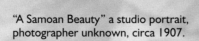

Card by an unknown publisher, circa 1907.

A Samoan Beauty

"A Samoan Beauty" a studio portrait, photographer unknown, circa 1907.

This portrait of a Samoan girl although shot in a studio setting is quite poignant. Published in Suva Fiji by A.M. Brodziak, circa 1910.

A SAMOAN GIRL.

Popular card published by the English firm of Raphael Tuck and Sons Ltd, art publishers to the King and Queen, circa 1910. The caption on the reverse is worth noting as it shows the prevailing views of the period. *"A Samoan Girl - "Fair Samoa" a group of lovely islands in the South Pacific. Natives light brown in colour, with splendid physique, and handsome regular features. The young women and girls are models of symmetry in form, with large eyes, oval faces, and pearly teeth. Their dispositions are bright and cheerful. They are clever cooks, and fond of stories and music. Their name for Robert Louis Stevenson was Tasitala - Teller of Tales."*

Scarce and unusual early advertising card put out by the Oceanic Steamship Company, circa 1900. Non-divided back.

SAMOAN GIRLS. THE ORIENT EXHIBITION.
Copyright: *London Missionary Society, 16 New Bridge Street, E.C.*
Picture Post Card Department   Rev. CHAS. H. VINE, Manager.

Rare and unusual exhibition card for the London Missionary Society "Orient Exhibition" held in London in 1908. At this exhibition natives were exhibited from all the Pacific Islands where the group had missionary outposts. Here the three young women are shown completely clothed with the mandatory *kava* bowl in the foreground. There is little left to the imagination, unlike the other more risqué cards of the period. Published by the society, which had its own picture postcard department.

Kava *increases vigilance, memory reaction time, relaxation, restful sleep, and muscle relaxation. It decreases feelings of nervousness, chest pains, headaches, and dizziness.*

SAMOAN GIRLS PREPARING KAWA.

A stunning image of young girls preparing *kava*. Published as part of the E.L. series by A.M. Brodziak Suva, Fiji, circa 1907.

Apia, Samoa

Samoan girl published by A.J. Tattersall Apia, circa 1910. Both local dress and recent imports are shown in this studio image.

Publisher unknown, circa 1910.

Above center:
Popular card published by the English firm of Raphael Tuck and Sons Ltd. - art publishers to the King and Queen, circa 1910. The caption on the reverse is worth noting as it shows the prevailing views of the period. "*A Samoan Beauty - to the English-speaking world the Samoan Islands are dear for Stevenson's sake. Seeking health, he made his home, under those blue skies where the beautiful scenery and charm of the natives delighted him. The language of this kindly and attractive race is soft and pleasant - the Italian of the Pacific - and their customary greeting is Talofa - My love to you!.*"

Published in Sydney by the firm of Swain and Company, circa 1900. Non-divided back.

A SAMOAN BEAUTY.

A Samoan Belle

Samoan woman

Published by Gos. Arnold, Suva, Fiji

Above right:
Published by Gus Arnold in Suva Fiji, circa 1910, here the topless woman is depicted in both traditional as well as western dress. Gus Augustus Arnold moved from Sydney to Fiji in 1904 and operated a tabacco, hairdressing, and fancy goods business located next door to the Pier Hotel in Suva. Although not a photographer, he purchased the rights from contemporary photographers, and not surprisingly his cards are often duplicated by other firms of the day. The company was sold, in 1911, to Vivian Hargrave, a long-time employee.

Right:
Published in Sydney by the firm of Swain and Company, circa 1900, this image has in the background a finely woven mat, which was an item of great prestige. Non-divided back.

A Samoan Belle

Samoan custom traditionally requires families and villages to offer passing visitors hospitality, often extending to overnight accommodations.

Copyright.

PAGO PAGO SIVA PERFORMERS.

A card depicting a pair of Pago Pago *Siva Siva* dancers complete with all their headdresses and other native garb. Published by HB publishers, London, circa 1900. Non-divided back.

8. SINGING GIRL, SAMOA.
Oceanic S. S. Co.

OCEANIC S S CO LINE TO HAWAII, SAMOA AND AUSTRALIA

Scarce advertising card for Oceanic Steam Ship Company, circa 1910. Entitled " Singing Girl Samoa," the artwork is by O.G. Coutts.

Published by the firm of Alfred John Tattersall, Apia, circa 1910. This image is from a negative by photographer John Kerry, circa 1880.

TWO BELLES OF SAMOA.

"Greetings From Samoa" a card typical of the period. Publisher unknown, circa 1910.

"Val. Samoa." A good example of a postally used card with handwritten inscription on front "*En Route to Australia Pago Pago Samoa June 16 06.*" The Samoan Islands were an important refueling and stopping off point en-route from the West Coast of the United States to New Zealand and Australia. Publisher unknown. Non-divided back.

Val. Samoa.

En Route to Australia Pago Pago Samoa June 16 06.

Rare named image by Thomas Andrew, circa 1904, this card depicts the *taupou* Leone who was a model in numerous cards published by his firm in Apia. Non-divided back.

TAUFOU LEONE T. ANDREW 1904 386

Taufou Leone

6358 Types Samoan Girls

Muir & Moodie.

Published by the New Zealand firm of Muir and Moodie, Dunedin, circa 1910. This is one of the few images showing Samoan women in traditional native garb without the addition of western clothing. Originally a studio portrait taken by Alfred Burton of the Burton Brothers in 1884 and 1885, it was part of the "The Camera in the Coral Islands" series. Upon the death of the Burtons, Muir and Moodie acquired all the firms negatives leading to the publishing of this card and many others.

Taupou of Tutuila.

Very rare card titled "Taupou of Tutuila" and carries the imprint on reverse "American Samoa Naval Station." This type of card may have been officially published for the United States Navy by the firm of Thomas Andrew, Apia, circa 1907.

Samoan Belles

Early card depicting three women in front of a *kava* or "grog" bowl entitled "Samoan Belles." Published in Sydney by the firm of Swain and Company, circa 1900. Non-divided back.

A Samoan Belle   S. M. & Co.'s Series   Sarony, Photo.

How's this Damsel

Almost comical, this card entitled "A Samoan Belle" was published in Saxony Germany for the firm of S and M, Auckland, circa 1900. Typical inscription of the time period, *"Hows this Damsel?"* Non-divided back.

Real photo postcard, circa 1915. Photographer unknown.

Samoan Lady Dancer. AJT 120

Real photo postcard of a *taupou* by Alfred John Tattersall,
Apia, circa 1907. Ink stamped on back "Samoa Postcard."

Real photo postcard, circa 1915 of a
taupou. Photographer unknown.

*Dutch explorer Jacob Roggeveen first sighted the islands in 1722. The French Admiral,
Louis de Bougainville, visited the islands in 1768. After seeing the inhabitants' prowess with
their numerous canoes, he named the group "The Navigator Islands".*

A Samoan Girl

A. M. Brodziak & Co., Suva - Fiji

Published by A.M. Brodziak in Suva Fiji, circa 1900. Brodziak was well known for his studio portrait cards of both Samoan and Fijian peoples. Non-divided back.

Gruss aus Samoa.

Published by the firm of Alfred John Tattersall, Apia, circa 1910. This image is from a negative by photographer John Kerry, circa 1880.

Greetings from Samoa.

"Greetings From Samoa" a card typical of the period. Publisher unknown, circa 1900. Non-divided back.

Published by Thomas Andrew, Apia, with printed inscription, 1916.

Published by Thomas Andrew, Apia, with printed inscription, 1910.

The present-day population of Samoa is approximately 180,000 people.

SAMOAN MAID

Would'nt YOU like to see SAMOA!

13

Real photo postcard, circa 1920. Photographer unknown.

Samoan Belles

Early card depicting three women in front of a *kava* or "grog bowl" entitled "Samoan Belles." Published in Sydney by the firm of Swain and Company, circa 1900. Non-divided back.

Published by Thomas Andrew, Apia, with printed inscription 1910.

F. T. Series. No. 524. SAMOAN GIRLS. PAGO PAGO.

Part of the "F.T. series," this was published in Saxony, Germany, circa 1900. Non-divided back.

A Samoan Beauty. A.T. Photo copyright 105.

Real photo postcard by Alfred John Tattersall, Apia, circa 1907. Ink stamped on back "Samoa Postcard"

Chief's pillows, like those of Tonga and Fiji, were traditionally made of wood or bamboo. Samoan legend relates that sleeping on hard surfaces gave Samoans their erect, strong, and straight nature.

Real photo postcard, circa 1920. In this image a woman is shown garbed in traditional bark cloth attire standing in front of a typical thatched dwelling or *fale*. Photographer unknown.

Real photo postcard card, circa 1920 of a impromptu *Siva Siva* dance. Photographer unknown.

The fastest tectonic movement on earth, 9.4 inches per year, is at the Tonga micro-plate near Samoa.

Real photo postcard, circa 1920. In this clearly staged *Siva Siva* dance the *taupou* is presented to the intended viewer in a naive and innocent way. Photographer unknown.

Real photo postcard, circa 1920. Photographer unknown.

Real photo postcard, circa 1915 of a *taupou*. Photographer unknown.

Real photo postcard, circa 1920. Photographer unknown.

"MISA"

(DON'T BE IMPATIENT!)

Real photo postcard, circa 1924 with inscription, *"Misa - (Don't be impatient)."* Photographer unknown.

Real photo postcard, circa 1920. Photographer unknown.

Real photo postcard, circa 1920 of a *taupou*. Photographer unknown.

Samoan Halfcaste

Real photo postcard, circa 1915 by the Rose Stereograph Company, Armadale, Victoria, Australia. Inscribed and titled "Samoan *Halfcaste*." In this studio portrait the *taupou* is holding a parrying shield from the Solomon Islands. Studio props such as this were commonplace, even though they had nothing to do with the area they are meant to represent. Exotic romanticism was all that mattered. George Rose started his firm in 1880 and was originally a producer of stereo cards. In 1908 he branched out with the production of real photo postcards. Views of Fiji, Samoa, New Zealand, and Australia were his specialty. The firm was active until 1925 with offices in Melbourne, Sydney, Wellington, and London.

Real photo postcard, circa 1930 - photographer unknown. Although carrying a pencil inscription of
"*Samoa*" on reverse it is more likely a studio image of a central Polynesian woman most likely from Tahiti.

LES BEAUTES POLYNÉSIENNES

8ª TURERE, Ile Raiatea (Iles-sous-le-Vent)

LES BEAUTES POLYNÉSIENNES

10, TETUANUI, Ile Borabora (Iles-sous-le-Vent)

Card from the "Les Beautes Polynesiennes" series by Lucien Gauthier photographer and publisher, circa 1907. Here a beauty from Bora Bora is pictured in a studio portrait that shows some apprehensiveness by the young model.

LES BEAUTES POLYNÉSIENNES

108 - TAHITI - Une beauté tahitienne
A tahitian beauty

Edit. L. Gauthier

Card from the "Les Beautes Polynesiennes" series by Lucien Gauthier, photographer and publisher, circa 1907. In this beautiful card a young woman from Raiatea is pictured in this studio setting.

Tahiti

Card from the "Les Beautes Polynesiennes" series by Lucien Gauthier photographer and publisher, circa 1907. Here a young girl from Raiatea is the photographers model.

LES BEAUTÉS POLYNÉSIENNES

4ª MARAA, Ile Raiatea (Iles-sous-le-Vent)

LES BEAUTÉS POLYNÉSIENNES

7ª TERAI, District de Pirae (Tahiti)

"Tahitian Beauty" by Lucien Gauthier photographer and publisher, circa 1906. This card shows the young girl wearing a traditional *pareau* of the time period.

Card from the "Les Beautes Polynesiennes" series by Lucien Gauthier photographer and publisher, circa 1907. Here a young girl from the district of Pirae on the island of Tahiti is pictured in a serene pose.

Chapter 6

Tahiti

No place on earth stirs the imagination as much as the islands of Tahiti. Ever since their discovery in the 18th century, the West has been fascinated with this idyllic paradise. The birthplace of "the noble savage" concept, Tahiti's fame was further enhanced in the late 19th century by artist Paul Gauguin, with the publication of the book *Noa Noa*. In it, he enhanced the perception of a heavenly paradise on earth, where sexual freedom was the norm.

The islands of Tahiti form two areas. The windward islands are principally centered, with the island of Tahiti being the most populated area. It is followed by the islands of Mo'orea, Me'etia, Tetiaroa (Marlon Brando's private island), and Mai'ao. The leeward islands are Raiiatea, Taha'a, Huaheine, Bora Bora, Tubuai and Maupiti. With the exception of Tetiaroa and Tubuai, they are "high islands," with volcanic cores surrounded by barrier coral reefs and crystal-clear lagoons.

The first European to set foot on the islands was the Englishman Samuel Wallis; his ship *Dolphin* anchored on June 17, 1767, at Taiarapu, on the island of Tahiti. He was soon followed by Spanish, French explorers, and of course Captain James Cook, who had a great affinity for the people and islands of Tahiti. The islands were again thrust to the center of attention in 1790, after the famous "Mutiny on the Bounty" incident under Captain Bligh.

As in other areas of the Pacific, explorers in Tahiti were soon followed by western missionaries, who had a profound influence on traditional native culture. These new arrivals took control of island politics and, after a series of wars between feuding tribal rivalries, the island chief Pomare became king. The French assumed control of the islands in 1842, under Queen Pomare's reign, with formal annexing occurring in 1880. Today, the islands remain under French control and make up the centerpiece of French Polynesia. The islands are heavily subsidized by France, as the main industries of tourism and black pearl farming are unable to meet the economic needs of the territory.

Tahiti, like other strategic islands in the Pacific, had a burgeoning colonial market in postcards and photographs. The first picture postcards were introduced to the islands by photographer and curio dealer, Charles George Spitz, in 1898. Later the same year, upon his father's death, George Spitz expanded the postcard business, using images taken by his father in the 1880s and 1890s. He was soon followed by the American jeweler, photographer, and curio dealer, Frank Homes, who began production in 1902. French photographer Lucien Gauthier came shortly after. Other photographers and publishers soon followed, but the early pioneers were responsible for the majority of the postcards issued prior to 1915.

Popular card by Frank Homes, Papeete, circa 1906. Vignette of Prince Hinoi who was also known as Pomare V along with the mandatory island maidens or *vahines* in the foreground.

LES BEAUTÉS POLYNÉSIENNES

2. MAREVA, Ile Tahaa (Iles-sous-le-Vent)

Left:
Card from the "Les Beautes Polynesiennes" series by Lucien Gauther photographer and publisher, circa 1907. A most unusual portrait due to the photographers concentration on getting the strong Polynesian features of this young woman from Tahaa by shooting her in profile.

LES BEAUTÉS POLYNÉSIENNES

8. MOO, Ile Moorea Oceanie

LES BEAUTÉS POLYNÉSIENNES

9. TERII, District de Papeete (Tahiti)

Right:
Card from the "Les Beautes Polynesiennes" series by Lucien Gauthier photographer and publisher, circa 1907. Here the young girl from Papeete is seen with plumeria flowers and a traditional shell crown.

A card from the "Les Beautes Polynesiennes" series by Lucien Gauthier photographer and publisher who operated from the Hotel Tiare in Papeete, circa 1907. Here a beautiful young girl from Moorea is captured in a sultry pose.

LES BEAUTÉS POLYNÉSIENNES

3. VIVIRANI, Ile Aratika (Pomotu)

Card from the "Les Beautes Polynesiennes" series by Lucien Gautheir photographer and publisher, circa 1907. In this card a young woman from Aratika in the Tuamotu Islands is shown in profile.

LES BEAUTÉS POLYNÉSIENNES

5. TURAI Punaavia (Tahiti)

Card from the "Les Beautes Polynesiennes" series by Lucien Gautheir photographer and publisher, circa 1907. In this card a young girl from the district of Punaavia in Tahiti is shown in a traditional *pareau* of the time peiod.

Tuane.

F. HOMES, TAHITI.

Early card by Frank Homes, Papeete, circa 1902. Non-divided back.

Noho.

F. HOMES, TAHITI.

Popular early card by Frank Homes, Papeete, circa 1902. Non-divided back.

COLONIES FRANÇAISES

ETABLISSEMENTS FRANÇAIS DE L'OCEANIE

Jeune femme en Costume de fête

Edition G. Spitz, Tahiti

38 - TAHITI. - Le Sourire Tahitien
A Tahitian smile

Popular image taken by the publishers father Charles George Spitz in the late 1880s. Publisher George Spitz , Papeete, circa 1906.

Card presumably published in France and part of a "Colonies Françaises" series. Publisher unknown, circa 1906.

E. HÄNNI, éditeur

TAHITI. - Un Trio dans la brousse

Extremely early card marked E. Hanni, editeur, circa 1900, non-divided back.

Pareau *is a traditional Tahitian woman's garment that can be worn in several dress styles, as a wrap, or as a skirt. Cotton cloth, boldly printed in Manchester, England, with tropical floral motifs, was imported by enterprising merchants to the Tahitian islands in the mid-19th century. It became extremely popular and fashionable there and was immortalized by Western painters such as Paul Gauguin, among others. Pareaus are still worn today throughout Polynesia.*

Tahitiennes.

F. HOMES, TAHITI.

Early and provocative image of the time period by Frank Homes, Papeete circa 1902. This is one of his earliest recorded photographs. Non-divided back.

Early card by Frank Homes, Papeete, circa 1902. Non-divided back.

Tahitienne, faisant une cigarette.

F. HOMES, TAHITI.

OCÉANIE FRANÇAISE
Vahine Tahiti

Card presumably published in France and part of an "Oceanie Française" series. From an original photo by Charles Georges Spitz, circa 1880s. Publisher unknown, circa 1910.

OCÉANIE FRANÇAISE
Vahine Tahiti

Card presumably published in France and part of an "Oceanie Francaise" series. From an original photo by Charles Georges Spitz, circa 1880s. Cards such as this, depicting topless women, are quite scarce and were a source of inspiration for the artist Paul Gauguin. Publisher unknown, circa 1910.

Early card by Frank Homes, Papeete, circa 1902. Non-divided back.

Vanilla is widely grown in Tahiti, having been imported into the islands in the early 1800s as a cash crop for export. It is a vine of the orchid family and grows best in interior valleys.

Group of young women making head crowns of scented flowers. Published by Lucien Gauthier, Papeete, circa 1910.

OCÉANIE FRANÇAISE
Teraaroa

Card presumably published in France and part of an "Oceanie Francaise" series. From an original photo by Charles Georges Spitz, circa 1880s. Cards such as this depicting topless women are quite scarce and were a source of inspiration for the artist Paul Gauguin. Publisher unknown, circa 1910.

1 — TAHITI - Une Vahine — A Vahine

Card published by G. Sage, Papeete, circa 1915.

A card showing popular dress of the period with a typical *pareau* cloth wrapped as a skirt. Published by George Spitz, Papeete, circa 1906.

A scenic view entitled "Papeete" showing the romance and exoticness of the island complete with the mandatory island maiden or *vahine* in the background. Published by Lucien Gautheir, Papeete, circa 1910.

32. PAPEETE (Tahiti)
Tahitienne allant au bain

"Native Women" published by Lucien Gauthier, Papeete, circa 1910.

TAHITI. - Papeete. - Femmes indigènes. - *Native women*
Edit. L. Gauthier - Papeete

Two young women from Raiatea with *pareau* wrapped as skirts. Published by George Spitz, Papeete, circa 1906. Members of the Spitz family were the largest purveyors of curios, photographs, and postcards in French Polynesia. Located on the waterfront area of Papeete, the store sold a vast array of "native curiosities." The firm closed its doors in 1948. Descendants still reside in Tahiti today.

19. Jeunes Femmes de RAIATEA (Iles-sous-le-Vent)

 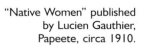

TAHITI - Papeete. - Deux beautés tahitiennes
Two tahitian beauties

Edit. L, Gauthier - Papeete

Edition G. Spitz, Tahiti

80. - TAHITI. - Vaiahu, une Tahitienne
Vaiahu, native girl

Left:
This girl whose name was Valahu
was one of the publisher's favorite
models. Published by George Spitz,
Papeete, circa 1906.
Far left:
"Two Tahitian Beauties" published by
Lucien Gauthier, Papeete, circa 1910.

98. - TAHITI. - La Toilette Tahitienne
The Tahitian Dress

57. - Aebo et Mere, Tahitiennes
Tahitian girls, Aebo and Mere

Edition G. Spitz, Tahiti

An enticing view by George
Spitz, Papeete, circa 1906.

Published by George Spitz, Papeete, circa 1906.

Tahitian is still widely spoken throughout French Polynesia but young people today communicate almost exclusively in French.

137

A card reminiscent of some of Paul Gauguin's reclining women paintings. Published by Lucien Gauthier, Papeete, circa 1910.

Tahiti is 2,400 miles southeast of Hawaii and is situated about halfway between South America and Australia.

Group of young women weaving hats. Published by Lucien Gauthier, Papeete, circa 1910.

Card published in France as part of the "Edition Marche Colonial" series. Publisher unknown, circa 1905.

Terii Vahine.

F. HOMES, TAHITI.

Early card by Frank Homes, Papeete, circa 1902. Non-divided back.

OCÉANIE FRANÇAISE
Maraa et Ariitai

Card presumably published in France and part of an "Oceanie Française" series. From an original photo by Charles Georges Spitz, circa 1880s. Publisher unknown, circa 1910.

OCÉANIE FRANÇAISE
Popoti Vahine

Tahitiens. - Caroline, Maraa et Terii

A trio of young Tahitian girls by Frank Homes, Papeete, circa 1910.

Card presumably published in France and part of an "Oceanie Française" series. From an original photo by Charles Georges Spitz, circa 1880s. Publisher unknown, circa 1910.

OCÉANIE FRANÇAISE
Vahine Tahiti

Card presumably published in France and part of an "Oceanie Francaise" series. From an original photo by Charles Georges Spitz, circa 1880s. Cards such as this depicting topless women are quite scarce and were a source of inspiration for the artist Paul Gauguin. Publisher unknown, circa 1910.

Iaorana *is the Polynesian greeting in Tahiti that means "good health."*

Real photo postcard by Max B. DuPont photographer, Papeete, circa 1926.

"The Fisherman's Daughters." Published by George Spiitz, Papeete, circa 1906.

"Two island maidens." Published by Lucien Gauthier, Papeete, circa 1910.

A view of two rather apprehensive young girls published by Lucien Gauthier, Papeete, circa 1910.

Tepairu.

F. HOMES, TAHITI.

An early card by Frank Homes, Papeete, circa 1902. Images like this were used by Paul Gauguin in painting some of his most famous works. Non-divided back.

Tuane.

F. HOMES, TAHITI.

Early card by Frank Homes, Papeete, circa 1902. The young woman here was one of the photographer's favorite models. Non-divided back.

*Breadfruit, or uru, was the mainstay of the ancient Tahitian diet. It was breadfruit that led the infamous Captain Bligh back to Tahiti. The English admiralty had sent him, in command of the **HMS Bounty**, to retrieve breadfruit for replanting in the Caribbean, thereby securing a cheap and plentiful nutritional food for the plantation slaves. The voyage ended in the infamous mutiny.*

56 — TAHITI - Deux jolies filles au cœur de la brousse — Two lovely girls in the middle of the scrub

Card marked "Edition R.P." on reverse. Publisher unknown, circa 1915.

Early card by Frank Homes, Papeete, circa 1902. Non-divided back.

Tahitienne.

F. HOMES, TAHITI.

30. – Une beauté tahitienne
A Tahitian beauty

Tahiti, Edit. L. Gauthier

Popular studio portrait of the time period. Published by Lucien Gauthier, Papeete, circa 1910.

TAHITI — Maire Maatea

Card published in France as part of the "Edition Marché Colonial" series. Publisher unknown, circa 1905.

TAHITI - Jeunes Filles endimanchées

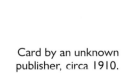

Card by an unknown publisher, circa 1910.

Moe et Tupura

Card by an unknown publisher, circa 1910.

Real photo postcard by Max B. DuPont photographer, Papeete, circa 1926.

TAHITI — Natua, la Perle Tahitienne

25. PAPEETE (Tahiti — Tahitienne se mirant dans l'eau)

Card published in France as part of the "Edition Marche Colonial" series. Publisher unknown, circa 1905.

French Polynesia covers a vast area of the southeastern Pacific, but its total landmass covers only 2,200 square miles.

An unusual view published by Lucien Gauthier, Papeete, circa 1910.

61 — TAHITI - Ainsi elles étaient autrefois !!. .
Such thery in former times !!...

Card marked "Edition R.P." on reverse.
Publisher unknown, circa 1915.

20 — TAHITI - Avant le bain — Before bathing

Card marked "Edition R.P." on reverse.
Publisher unknown, circa 1915.

39. · Aeho Vahine, Tahitienne
A Tahitian maiden (Aeho)

A beautiful card from a
photo taken by the
publisher's father,
Charles George Spitz,
in the late 1880s.
Publisher George Spitz,
Papeete, circa 1906.

175. PAPEETE — Tetuanui   TAHITI (Océanie)
Édition L. Gauthier — Papeete

One of the photographer's favorite
models, Tetuanui, is pictured.
Published by Lucien Gauthier,
Papeete, circa 1915.

28. - Jeune Fille indigène
A native young Girl

Card by an unknown publisher, circa 1910.

Édition G. Spitz, Tahiti

29. - TAHITI. - La Tahitienne — A typical Tahiti maiden

A beautiful card from a photo taken by the publishers father Charles George Spitz in the late 1880s. Publisher George Spitz, Papeete, circa 1906.

66 — TAHITI
Le Couvre-lit National "Tifefei"
The National bed quilt "Tifefei"

Card marked "Edition R.P." on reverse. An interesting handwritten inscription on the reverse reads *"This young girl hair is neater than most we saw. Odd that in a hot country hair should be both long and loose. The lava - lava is characteristic as the tifaifai (quilt). It looks woven but it is really painted on a sort of papery cloth made of palm or something."* Publisher unknown, circa 1915.

62 — TAHITI - Jeune, jolie et toujours souriante !...
Young, pretty and smiling ! ..

A card marked "Edition R.P." on reverse. Publisher unknown, circa 1915.

Card presumably published in France and part of an "Oceanie Francaise" series. Publisher unknown, circa 1910.

OCEANIE FRANCAISE
Blanchisseuses tahitiennes

The tradition of entertainment in ancient Tahiti centered on traveling performers called the arioi who sailed on great double hulled canoes from bay to bay and island to island, performing pantomime dramas and chants of a strong sexual nature. They usually performed in honor of Oro, their deity of peace, agriculture and fertility.

Tahiti Petites Danseuses tahitiennes
Little Tahitian dancers

TAHITIAN MAIDEN

A card published by Paul Normann, Papeete, circa 1925.

Real photo postcard, circa 1925. Photographer unknown.

Real photo postcard, circa 1920. Photographer unknown.

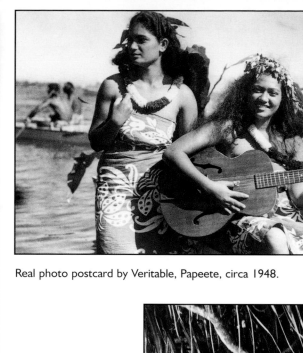

Real photo postcard by Veritable, Papeete, circa 1948.

Card published by Paul Normann, Papeete, circa 1925. This card shows the more burlesque version of the typical island maiden or *vahine*. This type of image was popular in both Tahiti and Hawaii in the roaring twenties.

Real photo postcard by Phil Mackenzie, Papeete, circa 1948. A beautiful photographic image that appealed to the aesthetics of the time period.

Real photo postcard, circa 1920. Photographer unknown.

Real photo postcard by Veritable, Papeete, circa 1948. In this rather late card, the models are wearing western swimwear inspired by Hawaiian "Aloha attire" of the period.

Real photo postcard by Phil Mackenzie, Papeete, circa 1948. A beautiful photographic image that appealed to the aesthetics of the time period.

World War One veterans Charles Nordhoff and James Hall moved to Tahiti in 1920 and made the "Mutiny on the Bounty" famous with their trilogy that was made by Hollywood into several film versions.

Real photo postcard by Veritable, Papeete, circa 1948.

Tahiti - Chanteuse

Real photo postcard, circa 1925. Photographer unknown.

149

Tahitienne. - TAHITI. - Tahitian girl

A card published by the Spitz Curio Store, Papeete, circa 1930.

A card by an unknown publisher, circa 1930. A short note typed on the reverse, "*In memory of days gone by 1933.*"

Vierges tahitiennes. - TAHITI. - Tahitian maidens

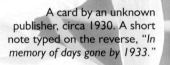

A card published by the Spitz Curio Store, Papeete, circa 1930.

Tahitiennes. - TAHITI. - Tahitian girls

Une Sirène Tahitienne. - TAHITI. - A Tahitian mermaid

A card published by the Spitz Curio Store, Papeete, circa 1930.

27 TAHITI Jeune tahitienne
Young tahitian woman

A card published by Paul Normann, Papeete, circa 1925.

Marlon Brando bought the beautiful island of Tetiaroa, in 1966, after falling in love with Tahiti and the people while filming a version of "Mutiny on the Bounty." He opened a small hotel there, in 1970, and had further plans for his island paradise, none of which came to fruition. The hotel is open to this day.

Tonga

Tongan Nativehouse

Tongan Nativegirls

Rare early pioneer card postmarked Nuku'alofa in 1900. Publisher unknown. Non-divided back.

Captain Cook named Tonga the "Friendly Islands" after his first visit in 1774, due to the hospitality of the Tongan people.

Chapter 7

Tonga

The Kingdom of Tonga, today, is composed of 172 islands with a population of approximately 110,000 inhabitants. The islands are small with a combined landmass of 269 square miles. Closely linked to its two close neighbors, Fiji and Samoa, it is culturally part of Western Polynesia, having been settled from nearby Fiji about 1200 B.C.

The islands form three main groups, the island of Tongatapu or "Sacred Tonga" gives part of its name to the entire group, its present day capital of Nuku'alofa lying to the south. To the north are the islands of Vava'u and in the center the many islands of Ha'apai. With the exception of the island of Tofua, with its large freshwater lake and active volcano, most of the islands are coraline in nature and low lying.

The first European to sight the islands was the Dutch entrepreneur Jacob Le Marie on a private expedition in 1616, followed in 1643 by the Dutch explorer Abel Tasman. But it was Captain James Cook who left us with the most detailed accounts visiting the group on his second and third voyages of discovery.

In 1799 the first missionaries arrived but soon left. This ill fated expedition by the London Missionary Society was plagued with strife and hostility as it was a time of great upheaval and war in Tonga between high-ranking rivalries which continued on for several decades. The Wesleyan missionaries, who arrived in 1828, converted George Tupou, who became King in 1852, to Christianity. He had the strongest influence in defeating the old order. As the king, George Tupou. by his independent nature, was able to keep Tonga free from direct annexation by the major maritime powers of the day. He accomplished this with the help and advice of missionary Shirley Baker. Through his guidance, treaties of mutual protection were signed at the end of the 19th century, the most important being the treaty with Great Britain.

Today, the Kingdom of Tonga is the only Pacific Island nation that has not been colonized by a foreign power. Its current monarch, King Tupou IV, is a remarkable man who governs his island kingdom with a firm hand. He has based his reign on traditional Polynesian values blended with Christianity and modern technology. Under the king's guidance, an importance is placed on the land, which can never be sold, thus helping to keep the deeply rooted Polynesian culture alive for future generations.

Early French advertising trade card, circa 1900 and part of the "Humanas Oceania" series.

KAVA CEREMONY, TONGA

Real photo postcard depicting young girls preparing *kava*. Printed in Great Britain, publisher unknown.

Tongan barkcloth, or ngatu, *is manufactured only by women and is an important item of cultural exchange.*

No. 418 *Tonga Girls throwing Oranges.*

GIRLS AT PLAY, JUGGLING ORANGES.   TONGA.

Popular image of the time showing young girls juggling oranges, circa 1900. Printed in Saxony Germany and part of the F.T. series #418. Non-divided back.

Early version on a popular juggling theme, circa 1900. Publisher unknown. Non-divided back.

Native Girl - Tonga

Beautiful image inscribed "Native Girl - Tonga," circa 1910. Real photo, publisher unknown.

Native Game of Fiji - Tonga 55

Unusual card showing young girls weaving although the handwritten description says otherwise, circa 1910. Real photo, photographer unknown.

Tongan Girl

A. M. Brodziak & Co, Suva - Fiji

Rare early card entitled " Tongan Girl" by A.M. Brodziak, Suva, circa 1899. An early producer of Fiji, Samoan, and Tongan postcards, Adolphus Meyer Brodziak arrived in Fiji in 1870 and had offices throughout Fiji. He ceased postcard production in 1911. An unusual depiction of a young Tongan girl. This image was considered quite provocative in its day, due to the strong missionary influence throughout Tonga at the time.

A Tongan Belle.

A poignant card entitled "A Tongan Belle," circa 1910. Marked on reverse "Friendly Island series, publisher unknown.

Greetings from NATIVE GIRLS, TONGA.

Card entitled "Native Girls Tonga," circa 1910. Here the young women are shown in missionary clothing with traditional Tongan ornaments. The young lady in the upper left corner does not appear to be too happy with having her photograph taken.

Tonga is unique as the only nation in Polynesia that continues in an evolved form, with a traditional social system yet a world-class position in the space age with TongaSat, The Friendly Islands Satellite Company.

Inscription on reverse, "*Tongans Vavau*," circa 1920. Publisher unknown.

Real photo postcard marked in pencil on reverse Tonga 1924. Although marked Tonga it would appear that this photo is from a Polynesian "Outlier" as a bare breasted view of Tongan women at this relatively late date would be improbable. Photographer unknown.

Real photo postcard by Nielen, Cincinnati, Ohio, circa 1920. Titled "In feast attire Nuku'alofa - Tonga Is."

TRADITIONAL LAKALAKA DANCE OF THE TONGAN ISLANDS

Real photo postcard depicting the *lakalaka* dance. Dance is an integral part of Tongan culture, society and history. Like other areas of West Polynesia the legs and lower body are used to keep rhythmic pulse. As with other islands of Polynesia, dance was a visual extension and enhancement of sung poetry based on complex arm movements either in a seated position or standing in one or more rows facing the audience, circa 1925, publisher unknown.